Mastering Our Mountains

Mastering Our Mountains

Jennifer Baker

Featuring Tamara L. Hunter,

(The First Global Next Impactor)
&
Other Award-winning Authors & Leaders

HAWAII WAY PUBLISHING

4118 West Harold Ct., Visalia, CA 93291

www.HAWAIIWAYPUBLISHING.com

For more information or to book an event contact HAWAII Way Publishing at HAWAIIWaypublishing@gmail.com, or call 559-972-4168
Printed in the United States of America
ISBN 978-1-945384-28-8

TABLE OF CONTENTS

Mastering our Mountains

Jennifer Baker

Mastering our Mountains is about that young person inside each of us facing the literal, or figurative, massive mountain in front of us. Every person has at least one of those mountains to scale. The more impactful your life is to become, the greater the size of the climb. As a young girl the mountains were my solace, they were the place that I could escape to, to sort out my thoughts and one of the few places that I was allowed to dream. Looking down on the valley below me made the huge challenges I was facing as a child seem smaller and more surmountable. Because mountains have always been my reprieve, I find myself looking at the greatest obstacles in my life as climbs to conquer and peaks to summit. As I push on, I am able to set my sites on the vista that awaits me, while enduring and celebrating the climb.

"As above, so below. As within, so without."

-The Emerald Tablet, Circa 3000 BC

Inside this book you will find stories filled with love and wisdom and directions that will hopefully challenge you and make you think. The stories may also seem familiar and synergistic. Once you discover the underlying theme within these stories, you will begin to understand the untapped power of your internal strength working in partnership with God, nature, source, then combined for unmatched power beyond most people's ability to comprehend. These simple instructions will help you overcome and achieve what most people would regard as impossible.

This book is dedicated from our hearts to you, for getting up every day, facing your mountain, and choosing to take that first step, over and over again until you get it right. If this book is in hand, your path to mastery was already open and there is a message within these pages intended for you to hear. Please take the time to read this incredible compilation of heart-centered stories and share them with others when you feel compelled.

My intention in creating *Mastering our Mountains* is to bring joy back to life and remind you that we are ALL created to be Y.O.U!

YOU + OUTSTANDING + UNIQUE!

It has been proven time and again that we are all individual, independent, and interdependent beings. Some will say for a reason, others say for no reason. Regardless, no one can argue that each human was born, live, and pass away with distinctive DNA. Upon conception, over three hundred thousand billion human variations could have achieved life, each different from the other. Out of those, YOU were born.

Celebrate your rarity!

Our brains are wired to find similarities, so we search for stories that we can resonate with. This stems from our human makeup. That's why we are drawn to those who have gone through something similar to ourselves.

The stories we have compiled for *Mastering our Mountains* should be used as an example, a learning lesson, a success tool, or wisdom to use as a guide map to your own unique situation. By finding similarities to whatever you are going through right now, you can gain insight and clarity into your own path. It then becomes your mission to tap into your brain's creative side to come up with an effective strategy for the specific mountain that you are facing.

Appreciate every journey, difficult situation, and critical thinking lesson. Without those, you cannot evolve into your full potential. It is your RESPONSIBILITY to be outstanding in your thoughts, actions, and feelings while pursuing your potential.

I became the woman of the house at a very young age due to an abusive, tumultuous childhood, and my parent's divorce. My story is not unique; it is similar to a significant number of families in America today. The difference was that my story didn't define me. Somehow, I knew all that I was going through didn't make sense, and this was not MY life story.

3

I was 40 years old when it hit me. I was sitting in the 7th row from a stage in a room of over 10,000 people gathered together for personal and business success, and when I realized that I was exactly where I was supposed to be. I was finally living my purpose without knowing it! At first, I was just a woman trying to do my best to help others with tools that I had found along the way. Today I am a small part of the world's positive change.

I still giggle like my inner child when I realize where I came from, and where I started. Every action I have taken has brought me to where I am today, to a place that child, living in that mountain valley, couldn't have ever imagined it. The greatest lesson I've learned was if I wanted something to change, it needed to start with me.

The ways and actions of wisdom are our witness to the world. –Jennifer Baker

My Life, My Mountain

Tamara Hunter

Have you ever heard three words that held enough power to change the course of your life? I have. Those three words, "You have cancer," can create fear, depression, anger, isolation, and so much more. I have heard these dreadful words as a granddaughter, a daughter, a sister, a mother, and for myself.

You never want to hear those words regarding your children. I know this firsthand. My daughter was 19 years old when I had to face the fact that she had a rare cancer. Thank goodness, she is a survivor. She is now married, with children of her own. She is happy, healthy, and living life to the fullest, with the 'mom car' that carries the sports equipment, dogs, and whatever else she requires for her wonderful, crazy life.

I can tell you this, it was not too difficult hearing those three words for myself. It was much easier than it was hearing them regarding my child, my mother, or any of my other family members or friends. By the time I was diagnosed, I had been through so much that cancer truthfully did not seem so bad. I did not cry once when I found out that my life was about to change… Again.

You see, I have faced some rather brutal stuff throughout my life. But, as tough as it was, I knew that I had to be tougher. If I told you everything, you would probably say something like, "Yeah, right. Next." So, I will share only a bit of my life experiences. Some of the events that shaped me into the strong woman that I am today.

Many believe that what I am about to tell you could be one reason why I ended up with breast cancer. It was the year 2000, I was married with four children and living in another state. To say I was in a happy marriage would be far from the truth. Little did I know when I married my husband that he was an undiagnosed, unmedicated, severe bipolar. So, one-minute things would be amazing and the next, I was in fear for my life. Some may say I was "walking on eggshells" but to me, it felt more like walking on glass.

Three years before, in 1997, I thought I was going crazy. I was experiencing huge swings and ranges of emotions. To borrow a line from *A Tale of Two Cities*, "It was the best of times and the worst of times." I had never been like this before but thought possibly after giving birth to my fourth child I may have changed. So, I started seeing a therapist three times a week. Yes, I thought I was nuts.

Within a couple of years, my therapist told me something that I will never forget. In fact, I remember everything about that

6

moment. Where I was sitting, where he was, what the room looked like, smelled like, and even how there was not that much light. He sat so stoic and calmly said, "Tamara, you are not crazy; in fact, you're perfectly fine. I believe you are married to an undiagnosed 'bipolar.'"

I did not even know what a bipolar was back then. I sure do now. But he went on to tell me what my choices were and how I should enlist those who knew and loved my husband for help. So, following his advice, I went about getting the help he needed for an "intervention" - at least I tried to.

To my surprise, no one believed me. Everyone that I contacted knew that I had been seeing a therapist for a couple of years. There became a pattern that I had to deal with for the next decade; I would tell the truth, and then I would be blamed for making up stories. In the beginning, when this started, I would document and prepare the facts; I was trying to save my marriage and family.

My husband became more and more violent after he was found to be bipolar. I was in a church that tried to keep families together and dealt with these types of matters behind the closed doors of leadership. I wanted to be a "good wife and church member" but, after over a year of more and more violence, I went to those leaders and told them that I valued my life and the lives of my children more than they valued my membership. I stood there, face to face and declared that I was leaving it all.

I escaped. That sounds dramatic. It was. In fact, many who know my story have been surprised that it has not been on some Lifetime Movie. Picture this: a police car, an undercover detective, grabbing basics, my children, our dog, and driving as fast as possible for the state line. When I had met with the judge who granted me the right to leave the state with my children, he warned me if my husband found out we were gone and could catch us, he could keep us until a judge would review the paperwork I had secured. Plus, my husband had threatened me that if I ever tried leaving, he would track me down, find me and I would no longer be breathing. It truly was 'run for your lives' time.

It was all planned, though not by me. I could not know the details. One morning I woke up in one state, in my beautiful house with custom furniture, designer this and that, an amazing view of the city, with friends and a community that knew and loved us. Next thing I knew, we were sleeping in a motel in another state, where one of my sons did not even have a pair of shoes. We left our home, most of our belongings, our church, the only life we had known, running towards the complete unknown, with only the hope of a better life without fear.

We only had what we were wearing and maybe a change of clothes with us. We would have to rinse out our undergarments each night. You see, we had a protective order in the state we left, but not in the state we fled to for safety. We had to wait until I could find an attorney who would help us receive protection. I had believed they would provide us with what we had risked so much to obtain, a new life.

There is so much more to this story. The protection did not hold. I still faced ongoing domestic abuse of all types. I was a single mother working three jobs all while raising three children with disabilities.

Life has a way of presenting us lessons and choices. I decided along the way of our new-found life that I would show up to each and every day with an attitude of gratitude. Believe me when I say that many times, I did not bounce out of bed saying, "Hey Life, here I am, give me another blow." I did, however, wake up and go over in my mind what I was thankful for each morning. This allowed me to see simple beauties, simple accomplishments, and simple treasures that the day before had brought. It also allowed me to see the beauty the new day was about to offer.

As I had stated in the beginning of this story, I heard "those three words" multiple times for immediate family members. Cancer is tough, there is no way of denying that, but that being said, I learned I was tougher. Life had prepared me in such a way I would never have expected. Through the challenges of the decades before my diagnosis, I had developed skills and acquired tools that taught me that I can handle anything.

My first day of treatment was December 10, 2014. I would not learn until years later that first day of chemotherapy was also considered my first day of recovery. Being the girl scout that I am, I brought everything on a long list of comfort items. Let's just say I had to be put in the corner so my bags would not be tripped over by the others in the chemo room. Once again, life decided I could use another lesson. Everything I brought with me could not have prepared for the events of that day and how it would redirect my entire future.

During my very first bag of chemo, I nearly died. I am not telling a tale here. I had a severe allergic reaction while sleeping. I woke to a voice asking if I was all right. As I tried to travel through the fog of sleep to that voice, I realized my face was on fire, my eyes were itchy, and my throat was tightening. I could not open my eyes and did not or could not answer. I knew at that moment I was anything but all right.

The voice that reached out to me in my darkness, that helped save me, belonged to a beautiful young girl at her mother's side. Her mother had happened to sit next to me that day. She would introduce us, and her mom would become the 'buddy' that I would travel my cancer journey with for the next three years. We became known as, "Double Trouble." Every infusion for a year and a half, every surgery, every follow up doctor visit, we did together, in one way or another. Our doctor and nurses noticed a change in the attitude of everyone around us due to the electric energy that our friendship created. We became "Chemo Buddies." Our relationship would become the model and foundation of the nonprofit corporation we would create together toward the end of 2017. Our foundation is called "Chemo Buddies for Life."

With my children now grown adults, I have found my life's purpose. The reason I had experienced and survived so many different types of trials. I realized that my mountains I had already climbed had trained me for this exact time. They had conditioned and taught me that I could do anything, but I also knew there is nothing that says it would be easy or fast. For me, it has not been either. Yet, I wake up each and every day with an attitude of gratitude to be building such a needed resource. I know that once built and fully functional, Chemo Buddies for Life will be able to help nearly everyone who so desperately needs this. Simply put, no one should ever face cancer alone.

Cancer is a dark subject, and it can hurt deeply when you keep seeing your family and friends move on to what I call Heaven. There is no denying that you can lose a piece of yourself when each new angel receives their wings. To continue our lives full of humor, hope, and heart, I needed to provide myself and those around me a way to see the positive. This is the best way I know not to give in to the "bad news" that we are bombarded with each and every day.

I traveled to a Summit in Phoenix midway through 2018 where I met a woman who challenged me with a year-long program, its name: "365 days of Awesome." I took that challenge. The challenge's rules were simple: create content of my choice and film every day for the entire year.

After consulting with one of my mentors, I created, "The Service Hero Program; 365 Days of Awesome; Celebrate Success Through Service." Every day, I would go on Facebook Live with a Service Concept or Service Hero. I had no idea what I was getting myself into or how it would be received.

Looking forward to each day, I dedicated myself to sharing my Service Heroes with an ever-growing audience. To my complete surprise, the good news and feel-good stories of people making such a difference in everyday life has gone global. I have been invited to speak to organizations within and outside of the United States.

Now I believe I was prepared for this moment in time to help those who have lost their way, those who are isolated, those who feel that they have been abandoned, and those who have nearly given up all hope. I am able to share without a shadow of a doubt that life is very much worth living.

My belief is that soon I will be sharing throughout the world that anything is possible, no mountain is too high, and all things can be overcome if you only believe. I do believe and because of that belief, today I woke up with an attitude of gratitude for my greatest climb. My life has been full of mountains, highs and lows, and beautiful vistas all along the way.

Lessons from the Trail

Craig Nielson

Mastering your mountain is a metaphor. It represents conquering a monumental task, overcoming a major obstacle or perhaps overcoming a major tragedy. The stories of the authors that follow are the stories of triumph and success when confronted with a mountainous challenge. These stories aim to inspire you and provide you with the tools to master your mountain. I have climbed many literal mountains throughout the Sierra Nevada, including Mt. Whitney, the tallest peak in the lower forty-eight states, and the iconic Half Dome in Yosemite National Park, where I have climbed to the summit five times. I love hiking and backpacking, and over the years I have covered over 600 miles of trail trekking through the wilderness, mostly in Yosemite.

As far as personal mountains that I have had to conquer, I have had a couple of major ones. The first was the hardest, most overwhelming, debilitating experience I have ever faced. At the age of twenty-one, I fell into a horrible depression so severe that I was hospitalized for three weeks. Full recovery from that experience took a lot of work, patience, faith, professional help…and exercise. These are certainly some of the same necessities required to master a mountain, real or otherwise. In my life, as well as in wilderness excursions I have experienced, I have had to use these same components to make it through the valleys and to the top of the summits. In doing so, I have identified some of the essentials needed for a successful ascent to *any* mountain.

The Approach

Making a successful ascent to any mountaintop requires planning and conditioning. You need to plan how to get to the trailhead, and you need to be in good enough shape to take on the physical challenge. I have also discovered the value of patience in getting to the trailhead, as well as in life. To get to a trailhead, you will likely travel on winding mountain roads that are slow going and your momentum is often hampered by a large, slow-moving vehicle that can never seem to find its way to a turnout.

I used to be very impatient when traveling mountain roads, always in a hurry to get to the trailhead, until one day I got popped for speeding and incurred a hefty fine. As with all things, I looked at this experience as a chance to learn, and the lesson I learned once again was: Be patient. Since then, I have committed to driving at the posted speed limit. Much to my surprise, I have found I am more relaxed when I drive, and I get to my destination in about the same time as if I had sped. Along the way, I also no longer miss out on the beauty of the climb. The same thing can happen along the trail. Even when I have been hot and miserable on the trail, my determination to make it to the summit urges me to press on. Making your way to the top of any mountain takes a great deal of patience.

Patience was critical to my recovery from depression, as well. I was in a very dark place and felt horrible. I wanted to feel good. Even though I was getting help and doing all the things I needed to do to get better, I often felt no different and wondered if I would ever feel good again. Therapy was expensive, and I went into debt. However, I took on the attitude that it would either make me or break me. I was committed to seeing it through. It took longer than I would have hoped, but eventually, I got there. Today, my life is filled with more love and joy than I ever expected. A life that was inconceivable to me back when I was depressed.

Any successful ascent to a mountaintop requires proper planning and preparation. First, you must know where you are going. Before I plan my trip into the wilderness, I spend time studying detailed topographic maps of where I want to go. These tell me the distance I need to hike plus the elevation gain I will need to climb to make it to the summit. With this information, I know how to create a training plan, so I am in adequate shape when I make the trip.

I also had to develop a plan for my recovery while I was in the hospital. In the hospital, everything was catered to me. I was cared for, all my meals were prepared for me, and no one needed my attention. I only had to concentrate on working the program and getting better. However, the reality was I would need to get back to functioning in the real world. So, I developed a plan to do just that.

First, I needed structure. I needed a reason to get up and get moving every day. I decided to start going to college and get a four-year degree. That was where I was going. I did not know what I would major in, but at least I knew I had something to occupy my time for the next four years. I also began cycling and would ride a few miles every day. On Saturdays, I planned all-day long-distance rides. In the hospital, I learned that when exercising, the body produces natural endorphins that act as an antidepressant. I wanted as much of that as I could get, so regular exercise became part of my plan. On Sundays, I committed to attending mass at church. Faith has been the foundation of my recovery. My mantra became "I can do all things in Christ who strengthens me" (Philippians 4:13). As with any challenge, you've got to believe you will succeed, you will weather the storm, you will make it to the top… eventually.

Getting Help

Over time and with a lot of consultation, I have evolved into a skilled, proficient mountaineer. In college, I took a backpacking class as an elective. In the following years, I have read many books, attended workshops at our local recreational equipment store to learn the newest trends for gear, and talked to many people with experience in recreating in the wilderness. Before I set off on the trail, I consult with the rangers at the ranger station where I get my permit and get informed of the trail conditions and anything else I should be aware of.

As for my recovery, I got outpatient help with a psychologist, I attended group therapy for several weeks after being released from the hospital, and I met often with the school counselor at the Junior College where I began attending classes. I also joined a young adult group at church for spiritual support.

I would go on to eventually earn a master's degree in Counseling and Educational Psychology. College Student Development was my emphasis of study. Years later, I started teaching Educational, Career and Personal Development at my local Junior College. Here, and within my coaching practice, I have discovered that help is one the most underutilized resources people have at their disposal that they will often avoid.

In my class, there was an exercise where students were questioned how they felt when someone asked them for help.

Most would respond they would be happy to help. Helping others would make them feel good. But when they were asked how they felt when they needed to ask someone for help, most responded that this made them uncomfortable. They said things like: "I don't want to bother them, I don't want to impose, I don't want to appear weak for something I should probably be able to do for myself." My response to these comments was, "How do you know if the person you're asking for help from doesn't feel like you do, when you're asked for help? Maybe they too are actually happy to assist, and when they help you it allows them to feel good about being able to do so."

Once before class, as I always did, I asked the class if they had any questions about anything we had covered before or that had come up while doing homework. A young lady in the back of the room raised her hand. I called on her and she said, "I know you're going to think this is stupid, but...?" I responded by saying, "Shame on you. Shame on you for imposing judgment on me and assuming I would think your question was stupid." I was being facetious. I continued, "I don't think your question is stupid and the answer to your question is..." I then asked the class how many other students had the same question and at least four others raised their hands. I made a teaching point out of it. I then said, "Now, by having the courage to ask the question you thought was 'stupid,' not only do you get the answer you needed, but you benefited four other students who had that same question."

In more recent years, I have been in the company of many successful people. For me, it can be intimidating, but I am not afraid to ask them a question, solicit a suggestion, or ask for some advice or help in general. Sure, there have been some who just want to tell you what you want to hear and do not follow through, but by far the majority have been happy to help. In my experience, asking for help has never been detrimental to me in any way. I have also learned you won't *get* help… unless you ask for it.

Obstacles and Unpredictability

As with any endeavor, obstacle, or setback, unpredictability can occur. You must be flexible and ready to adapt to make it through. Along the trail, I have encountered many obstacles. On one particularly memorable trip, we were trekking through a remote area in the northwest region of Yosemite. The trail in this remote section of the park was not maintained very well, and we came across a very large tree that had fallen across the trail. It was in a tight spot, so there was no going around it. The solution – We popped off our backpacks and hurled them over the tree. Then we climbed through the tree to the other side. Except for a few minor scratches and getting a little sticky from the sap in the tree, we made it through to the other side and continued on our way. On another trip in the Hoover Wilderness coming over Rock Island Pass, the switchbacks on the other side were covered by a major snow drift. This area was very steep, and we had to make our way down. Walking in the snow was way too slippery. The solution - We took our backpacks and sent them sliding down the hill. Then we too sat down on our backsides and slid down the snowdrift like being on a slide. It was actually quite fun.

When you encounter obstacles and setbacks, keep looking for a solution. When problems arise, ask yourself, "Where is my opportunity in this? What can I learn from this?" In the early days of my recovery, I went out for a very long bike ride. I was living in Southern California at the time, and this would be a ride from my home out to the ocean and back. The majority of the ride was along the San Gabriel Riverbed. This is a concrete riverbed that runs all the way from the San Gabriel Mountains to the ocean at Seal Beach. The bike path runs along the top edge of the riverbed. It could sometimes get crowded with other cyclists and pedestrians, so this bike path was not always conductive for a quick ride. I wanted to ride at an accelerated pace, so I took the ramp down into the riverbed where it was wide, smooth concrete and free from the others up above on the trail.

I needed to ride fast because I was feeling restless. Thoughts in my head were filled with negativity, and I started to become overwhelmed with anxiety. Riding fast was my way of imagining

I was trying to outrun my negative thoughts. I was riding at a very fast pace when up ahead I noticed a wide, flat stream of water, very thin like a film on the concrete, flowing from the sewage treatment plant into the river in the middle of the riverbed. I did not think of it as a hazard as I had ridden across wet ground and puddles before without incident. However, unknown to me and what I could not see, was a thin layer of algae growing on the surface of the concrete beneath the water.

When I crossed the water, it was slick as ice. The wheels of my bike immediately slid to the right, and I fell to the left in a brilliant crash. I managed to get my right foot unclipped from the toe clip, but my left foot remained stuck in the pedal. I stretched my left hand out to catch my fall and hit the ground with my left hand and left hip as I slid into a half circle before coming to rest. I freaked. Then in an explosion of frustration, I unclipped my left foot and shoved the bike from me, then unclipped my helmet, took it off, and threw it as I shouted the F-bomb as loud as I could. I then sat down on the ground and buried my face in my hands. I lashed out at God, "Why does this have to be so hard?" I sat for a few minutes to calm down. As I sat, what came to me was, "be still, and know that I am God... I am here." (Psalm 46:10) A calm came over me, and I then proceeded to assess the damage. I was pleasantly surprised that I was not at all seriously injured. Except for some slight pain on my left hip and a minor scuff of road rash on my left knee, I was fine. There was nothing broken or bleeding. The palm of my fingerless riding glove on my left hand had a hole worn through it, as did the left side of my spandex biking shorts. Other than that, I was perfectly fine. The damage to my bike consisted of a small scuff on the rear derailleur and left pedal. The handlebars were crooked, but I was able to straighten them again by wedging the front wheel between my legs and turning the handlebars with arms. All was okay. Given how fast I was traveling, it certainly could have been worse.

Obstacles, setbacks, and unpredictability usually are not as scary as they initially appear. Like my assessment after the bike wreck, when I initially looked at how extensive the snow drift we were going to slide down was, I was ready to turn back the way we came. After remaining calm, using careful assessment, and a prayer, I changed my mind and forged ahead. When faced with any dilemma, remain calm, focus on the solution, look for the opportunity, and tap into your higher power.

Embrace Being Uncomfortable

Being uncomfortable places you outside your comfort zone. This is where personal growth happens. If you keep doing what you are doing, you can expect to continue to get the same results. The trail can be anything but comfortable. Depending on the time of year, it can be hot. It can be dusty, and as you sweat, the dust sticks to you. Your muscles can start to ache, and you may develop a blister or two on your feet. It's all part of the process of getting to where you want to be. In the thick of it, you may feel like crap, like when I run a marathon (I have done five of them). Usually, at about the 24th mile, my thought process goes to thinking, "There is something sick and twisted about this" as everything in my body wants to stop, but my mind keeps it pressing on. Then awhile after crossing the finish line, I think, "That wasn't so bad."

Don't let being uncomfortable influence you to quit, or to not even start, for that matter. I used to be very quiet and painfully shy. I mentioned when I started college that I had no idea what I would major in. After I completed my first year, I took a speech class as one of my general education requirements. On the first day of class, the professor told us public speaking was the number one fear people have. Right then, I declared my major as Speech Communication. I figured if that were true and I could master public speaking, then I could do anything. Getting up before an audience and speaking terrified me in the beginning. I still get nervous before I go on to speak. But I have done it enough to know there are no negative repercussions for doing it. It still makes me uncomfortable, but I do it anyway.

Focus

I just mentioned how uncomfortable being on the trail can be. There are times when I have been miserable on the trail. Once, I worked so hard and over-hydrated, causing myself to be sick. When I climbed Mt. Whitney from Whitney portal with a full backpack up to base camp at 12,000 ft., I felt horrible when we got there. I went to bed that night wondering how I would ever make it to the top the next day because I felt so awful. Fortunately, a good night's sleep can work miracles. In the morning, after going to bed feeling terrible, I felt renewed and ready to go again. I made it to the summit with no problems.

That brings me to point out the need to reset when you are feeling down and discouraged. Each day presents a new beginning. It gives you the chance to rework your plan and redirect your focus. What you focus on will determine your experience. If I only focused on my discomfort and how miserable my body felt for a short time along the trail, I would never venture out. To make it to the summit of the mountain, you have to continue to focus on the goal. It is also important to focus on the beauty of the forest, wildflowers, lakes, rivers, dynamic geological features, wildlife, and of course the stunning views. This is what keeps me going in spite of how I feel along the way.

Perseverance

Never give up. Perseverance is key. Dig in when you feel as though you want to quit. Carrying on is the only way to make it to the top of your mountain. There were many times while working through my recovery from depression where I felt like giving up. Times that I thought perhaps I just was not meant to be happy. I thought maybe I would never get better. Many times, I felt like quitting school because it felt too hard and all the time I spent studying was not any fun. Sometimes I prayed and felt as though God was ignoring me. But despite all this, I did not let how I felt at the time stop me from continuing to do the things I had put in my recovery plan. I continued to work at them, continued going to school, and continued to pray. James 1:12 tells us, "Blessed is the one who perseveres under trial because, having stood the test, that person will receive the crown of life that the Lord has promised to those who love him."

Grit

Grit is something deep inside. It is that stuff that keeps your drive alive when you otherwise feel spent. Grit is what drives perseverance. It is what kept me stuck in a library late at night doing schoolwork and what got me up and out on my bike on Saturday mornings when all I wanted to do was stay in bed. I have seen it in the students I have taught, like the single mom working

26

nights and going to school to make a better life for her and her children. It comes from a burning desire to succeed. As I once heard a young lady who won the Dean's Award speaking at her graduation say, "Once I figured out I could do this, I never wanted anything so bad in my life."

Success happens from doing what needs to be done, *especially* when you do not feel like doing it. Sometimes climbing a mountain is a trudge. So is taking on the challenges of life. As you take one step forward on the trail, your view really does not change at all. Nevertheless, you are in fact one step closer to the summit. This is important to know when you are taking on a monumental task. Results do not happen overnight. Grit is the magic ingredient that keeps you climbing and gets the job done. If I could bottle it, I would make a fortune. But I also believe I do not need to because we all have it in us; we just have to dig deep and grasp onto it.

The Summit

Achievement is sweet, and from the top of a mountain, you look beyond to see many more peaks and valleys. When I see this view, I am reminded that in life there is not just one summit to reach, there are many. What I have been through on my road to full recovery from depression, I have applied to other challenges in my life. I have built a seven hundred square foot addition on to my home, having never built anything before in my life. I wanted to quit and hire someone else to finish, but I kept at it and eventually, I finished it.

During the economic downturn between 2008 and 2010, I was laid off from my job after serving thirteen years with the police department. This was my second greatest life challenge. What do you do when you have built a thirteen-year career, feeling set for life with good benefits and good retirement? I took my collective life experience, along with my education, and created a coaching practice dedicated to helping women who are hard on themselves and feel stuck, anxious, and frustrated. Even if they are immensely successful in one area of their life, they can feel like other areas really suck. I coach them to become incredibly confident in all areas of their life, so they can feel relaxed and secure no matter what. (If you want to learn more about that part of my story you can read about it in my other book, *Launch. Let Your Setbacks Propel You Forward.*) Today, I also teach backpacking and hiking in the Sierra Nevadas at my local Junior College; it is my favorite recreational activity.

From my current mountaintop, I can look back at all I've gone through. It has been a great ride and an awesome climb, filled with lots of roadblocks and challenges, but also with much love, joy, and happiness. If you had told me back when I was severely depressed, I would have the life I have today, I would have told you that you were smoking crack. Though I still have a long way to get to where I want to be and have new goals far ahead on my horizon, from where I stand now, it is a pretty great view. In the stories that follow, I hope you find your way to conquer your mountain. What may seem insurmountable, I hope you discover that it is possible, and find within you the power to make it to the top.

To read more in detail of my recovery from depression, look for my soon to be released book, *Love Is Our True DNA- A Testament to God's Healing Grace.*

Finding Joy in the Journey

Kim O'Neal

March 24, 2016, the words "You are a mess," echoed from my husband's doctor's mouth. "Stage four colon cancer is everywhere. Terminal." The words felt like bricks dropping from the sky, landing with a pounding thud on the unsuspecting pavement below. Jeff and I looked at each other; he saw the fear in my eyes and reached for my hand. I knew what he was thinking. He was not thinking of himself - Jeff never thought of himself. He was thinking of the kids and me.

Jeff's demeanor was calm as he began asking the doctor about his prognosis. The doctor was caring and began consoling the two of us as he told us that Jeff had three to four months to live.

My thoughts began to race; I was overwhelmed with fear. 'How can I do life without my partner and best friend? What will we say to our children? Who will walk our daughter down the aisle?' These thoughts continued to snowball in my mind. 'How will I be there for Jeff, this man that I love more than life itself? Will I be able to find the strength to be there for our two precious children? How will I balance everything and still take care of myself? Was I going to be able to watch my husband's body begin to deteriorate?' Anxiety began to consume me.

While Jeff continued talking, the doctor began to offer him anxiety and depression pills to ease the blow. All I could do was bolt for the car! Running out of the doctor's office, I was in a fog. My mind was numb, and I vaguely heard the office staff tell me to have a nice day.

Nine years prior, I had lost someone who was very dear to my heart. My grandmother and I were extremely close. I recall staying at her house a few weeks in the summer as a child, and she would come to our house and stay with us too. When it became too hard for her to live by herself, we moved her three hours from her home closer to ours. This was a very hard transition for her. She was leaving behind the house that she raised her two girls in as a single mom. It was not just a house, but a home full of memories.

After moving her a few blocks from our house, our relationship started to grow deeper. I was now a teenager. We understood each other's jokes, shared secrets that no one else knew, ate ice cream while watching *Jeopardy* and *Wheel of Fortune* and laughing with each other because we did not know the answers to the game shows.

As a few more years went by, her little old body was worn out. Grandma passed away, and I did not know how to handle the emptiness in my heart, nor did I know how to be there for my family. Deep depression consumed me for close to three years. Eight months of those three years, I only got out of bed a few hours a day. I remember lying in bed, listening to my husband playing with the kids and hearing them laugh in the living room, yet there was no desire to join them. This pain I felt inside broke my heart, and I began asking myself, "Would it be better if I was not here? What kind of damage is this causing my family by lying in bed all the time, missing out on their sweet lives?"

There was an inability to trust God with all my fears, worries, sadness, and frustration, thinking my troubles were too big for God to handle. Now I was facing a new harsh reality: This time it had to be different.

I remember running to the car, feeling as if my legs would barely carry me. They felt as heavy as cement. Life became a silent tunnel, and I was numb. Facing fear, doubt, and discouragement, my mind became an ocean of thoughts, emotions, pain, and dizziness. Wave after wave was crashing over me then pounding down my emotions; nothing felt stable or comfortable. The only truth was the next wave that would break would allow me to catch my breath. I began to cry out, saying, "Lord, please help me, I can't do this, this is too much for me to handle. I need you!"

Suddenly, I heard God say, "Then trust Me with your problems." I then experienced the security and grace of knowing I was momentarily safe in the arms of Jesus. Within days, our battle fighting this ugly beast had begun. We were traveling three hours every other week for treatments down in the Los Angeles area. Jeff and I stayed in hotels for five days a month while he received treatment. This gave God the opportunity to stir our hearts to date and love like we had never loved before. We would go out for dinners, sit by the hotel pool, play cards, go to the movies, and we even went to Disneyland a few times since we had season passes.

As the waves continued to crash, I could have chosen to stay drowning in the image of life's assaulting ocean, but I didn't. Keeping my head above water, I frantically began searching for hope. The realization of clinging to my faith in Jesus Christ was clearly evident; God was my lifeboat. I knew I needed Him to rescue me in the midst of this storm. "Trust me this time," He beckoned me from the waters. Through the pain, I had to choose to embrace the miracle of each moment and receive the gifts that God had for me each day. Experiencing life in new ways, regardless of our situation. I chose not to give in to depression like I had when my Grandmother died. Looking for grace to survive, I began to grow while amidst this tragedy. I began choosing life!

"God can restore what is broken and change it into something amazing, all you need is faith." Joel 2:25

Life has not been easy, but life is a choice. When Jeff and I were in hotels and doing chemo for those five days a month, we were away from our kids, and I had a lot of time to ponder my thoughts. One never thinks they will be in this situation, fighting this ugly beast. I often wondered what God's plan for the future was. I would go back to the times when our lives were full of laughter and things were enjoyable. When I came out of my previous depression, Jeff and I felt called to open our home and become a foster family to needy children. This was a family decision, and we knew this would be very difficult emotionally because these children would arrive with their pain from the past. Jeff and I had an ability to love these children. Children are a blessing from God, and we were blessed to have a beautiful home to offer them. Our family of four had a lot of love to give.

Once, I recall, Jeff and I were in the backyard packing our trailer to take our kids camping on our annual church camping event, when our phone began to ring. "Good evening Mr. O'Neal, we have a sibling set of two little boys, ages 18 months and 3 years of age. Could you possibly take them?" We were informed by the Social Worker that the 18-month-old was deaf, so this could be a little difficult, since we did not know any sign language.

Jeff and I discussed how to go camping and take two little boys who did not even know us. After discussing this with our children, our daughter of course said, "Yes! This will be fun, and I will help." At this time, our daughter was 10 years old. We were not sure how much help she would be. However, the decision was made, so we picked the boys up the next day. Our son was fourteen at the time, and the three-year-old immediately bonded to him, and he became his best friend. The camping trip was interesting, to say the least. With two brand new children who did not know us and did not know   if they could trust us, nor had they ever been in the mountains before.

Without hesitation, our family of four became a family of six. I began to learn sign language, took this little boy to a hearing specialist, since he had never been to one, and started the ball rolling to help these little ones. Our love for these two was strong, and our family created so many memories. We observed a little boy full of fear turn into a boy who learned how to communicate using sign language and began laughing and enjoying life. The three-year-old became a boy full of life and confidence. He had become so caring and compassionate towards others. Watching God transform these little boys right in front of our eyes was one of the most beautiful things we had ever seen.

Knowing the boys were up for adoption was difficult; however, we also knew in our hearts that God did not call us to adopt. Our job was to be a safe place of transition. We were called to love on these children until their adoptive parents were found. As this day approached, we began praying for the perfect family to love these two precious boys.

A few weeks later, Jeff was driving to work and received a phone call from a friend he had worked with. They had not spoken for quite some time. The conversation went on like any normal conversation, but Jeff began to ask some various questions. "What have you and your wife been up to lately?"

"Well, not a whole lot, but we have actually started the process to adopt."

Jeff replied, "Adopt, really? That's awesome. Have you already met the children, or what is the process?" His friend replied, "No, but we are asking for a sibling set of two. Both my wife and I learned sign language when we were younger, and we are hoping to adopt a deaf child."

As you can imagine, the phone got really quiet as my husband continued, "I don't know if you know this, but Kim and I are foster parents to two little boys, and one of the boys is deaf. They are up for adoption." Silence came over the phone; it was extremely quiet during this time. Both men were speechless!

The process started, and this couple met the boys. There was an immediate bonding, and they fell in love. They became a family of four six months later. This journey started our two years of being a foster family. We were blessed to have fostered 28 children that stayed in our home at different times.

After Jeff's diagnosis, we had to stop the process of being foster parents. It was an emotional blow because it was such a passion of ours. I did not understand why this was happening when all we desired was to offer these children who had no families love and a home. Our parents even stepped up and treated these children as their very own grandchildren.

Once again, those questions began flooding my mind. "Why would God take away such a happy and loving way to reach out to children who were hurting, and why was Jeff struck with something so evil?" I began to ask these questions over and over. But God continued to remind me that He was not doing this to cause pain, but I needed to look and search for Him amidst the suffering. It was what He was doing and not what He was taking away.

When chemo started, it hit Jeff incredibly hard. Wounds developed on the bottom of his feet and in his mouth, and he also had to battle through blood poisoning. After just the first round I was worried that I could already lose him.

At this time, Jeff and I met with a team of researchers that informed us that they had been working with nutraceuticals that might be beneficial to Jeff while going through his treatments. This plan included extremely powerful nutrients. They explained that they would help Jeff get through hours upon hours of chemotherapy and could help protect him from the damage that chemo may do. We began this product after his first round of chemo, and the sores in his mouth and feet went away in a matter of days. We couldn't believe it and didn't know what to think.

After Jeff's fourth round of chemo, he was playing full-court basketball, and he felt amazing. He also never lost his hair! After completing 1,000 of hours and 20 rounds of chemo he still looked amazing, felt incredible and people would constantly tell him that he looked the picture of health! No one would ever have known by looking at him what his body had been through, or that he was still battling stage four cancer. He was constantly educating others on how they could get through their own cancer battles too. He also led the youth group at our church and had a huge following of people who kept up on his journey and all his raw, inspirational posts. He taught everyone around him to "Love like it's your job!"

However, when the tumor in his colon started to break up and Jeff began to urinate pieces of tumor, it caused pain and inflammation in his bladder. To rectify this, we had to have surgery to clean the bladder out, and we had the rest of the dying tumor cut out of the colon. His colon that had been riddled with tumors was now completely clear, however the surgery was extremely hard on him and things did not go well. He started to decline very quickly. Things kept getting worse rather than better.

Jeff was the biggest fighter I have ever met. He never took any pain medication, took care of his body, and still praised God even through his trials and intense suffering. Jeff became very fragile. Walking became too difficult for him, so I was helping him get dressed and shower. The couch became his life, but he never stopped loving others and never complained. He knew God allowed him to have this cancer for a reason. Jeff would say, "It is an honor God chose me." Jeff was still leading people to Christ and to healing all throughout his battle. He was even helping marriages and struggling teenagers all from his couch. Jeff would say, "As long as I have air in my lungs, God has a plan and a purpose for me here."

God took Jeff home on February 18, 2018, and he was persistent and consistent until the end. The last week of his life our house was full of streams of people who came to love on Jeff and try to let him know the impact he had on their lives. Especially the youth of our church. They all came and sang and cried and laughed with Jeff. He was a second dad to so many of them, especially to those without a dad. You see, Jeff did not lose his battle to cancer, HE WON HIS BATTLE! My husband is in the arms of our Lord, and he is rejoicing and celebrating all that he deserves.

This has been a very difficult uphill journey for our family. Losing the man that I would lay down my life for is something I never thought I would go through, especially at the age of forty-four. My heart breaks for our two children, Natalie, age sixteen and Nick, age nineteen. They had to watch the strongest man they knew, their best friend, provider, counselor, protector, their father fight this battle. They watched him deteriorate before their eyes. Jeff would say, "I don't know what is worse, me going through this or you guys watching me go through this."

Life can bring us obstacles. The loss of a loved one, divorce, loss of a job, financial hardship, pain from your childhood are all difficult scenarios. There are times we do not know if we will make it through the day. Some of the days, we can barely get out of bed, but then there are days where we feel like we can run a marathon. Life is a choice; I choose life! Even through all the struggles and obstacles I have faced, I have chosen to trust God, make the decision to climb the mountain, and get to the top. I will be stronger than I have ever been before and be an overcomer. God tells us in Matthew 17:20, "Faith can move mountains."

If I keep my eyes focused on Jesus, it is easier to no longer look at what I don't have, and instead I look at what I do have. It has been a blessing having Jeff for twenty-two amazing years. He gave me the best gifts ever: Nick and Natalie. Jeff taught me how to love, trust God, be bold with my faith, and love others more than myself.

Jeff's final words to me were, "Kimberly, you are stronger than you think. I am so proud of you, and you can do this." He said this with such a strong voice and with so much clarity. Jeff never spoke again. I know that was God speaking through him, and because of those words, I can climb to the top of that mountain and overcome this pain, because I know I still have Jeff walking with me and my Heavenly Father to carry me.

"I waited patiently for the Lord to help me, and He turned to me and heard me cry. He lifted me out of the pit of despair, out of the mud and the mire. He set my feet on solid ground and steadied as I walked along. He has given me a new song to sing, a hymn of praise to our God. Many will see what He has done and be amazed. They will put their trust in the Lord. Oh, the joys of those who trust the Lord." Psalms 40:1-4

My Inner Super Strength

Chase Savanna Marmolejo

I often close my eyes and can picture myself with my little legs hanging off a bench on "Wisteria Lane," as I sit next to my favorite comedian, Ray Romano, while filming a commercial; or walking the Red Carpet with Selena Gomez as lights flash and cameramen yell for me to tell them my name. I can envision myself hugging Taylor Lautner and meeting most of the Disney stars I have always watched on TV. I also see myself on a shopping spree with Audrina Patridge, for MTV and then donating everything we purchase to charity.

I can see myself swimming with dolphins, or yelling, "Move that Bus!" as a family gets their first view of their "Dream Home." I am overwhelmed when I think of myself standing on stage in front of a giant cake at Disney World. After speaking in front of over 3,000 people, I can still hear them singing "Happy Birthday" to me!

Over the past years, I constantly have to pinch myself to see if this is all a dream, but while serving as a National Spokesperson for both "Make a Wish" and "St. Jude Children's Research Hospital," all of these "dreams" have come true. Especially my dream of helping other children. I have had the honor of playing a role in campaigns that have raised over $100,000 for "Make a Wish" and over $30,000,000 for St. Jude!

However, it did not start out as a dream. At first, it was a nightmare that I wished so much I could wake from. "This can't be happening... You have the wrong girl... You just said I was perfectly fine five minutes ago!" These thoughts rattled anxiously through my ten-year-old mind as I sat on the hospital bed, squeezing my mom's hand.

It was only a few weeks before that I had been running around on the playground with my friends. I had also been experiencing major headaches and several episodes of vomiting. One night, I woke up in a panic and ran to the bathroom. I barely made it there in time before I began continuously throwing up. I could hardly make out the words as I called for my little brother to "GET MOM!"

The very next morning, I cheerfully woke up my mom telling her I was ready for school. Even though I felt fine, something didn't seem to sit well with my mom, and she decided to take me to the doctor instead. When we got to the doctor's office, they could barely find my chart because of how rarely I had had to come in. After explaining everything to my doctor, he told my mom and I that I was probably suffering from the onset of migraines, and that we should journal the headaches and see him in a month. But right before we left, he said he would call us that night to see how I was doing. He had never done this before, but we didn't think much of it.

That night, my stomach had settled, but I was having excruciating headaches that would not seem to go away. When my Dad got home from work, I asked him to say a prayer for me. In this prayer, my dad said, "Please give us strength and help the doctors to be inspired to know what to do." We all found this a little strange, because at the time, we all thought I probably just had the flu, or possibly migraines.

Soon after, my doctor called to check how I was doing. My mom explained that my stomach was fine, but that I was complaining about my head. He stopped for a moment and then said, "Let's get her into the E.R. for a C.A.T. scan." My mom found this odd and told my dad what the doctor had told her. Then, thinking about what my dad had just said in his prayer, they quickly got me and my siblings into the car and headed for the emergency room.

Once there, we had to wait awhile before I was allowed to go back. During this time, my headache subsided, and I was returning to my upbeat self. I was passing all the neurological tests they gave me with flying colors. All the doctors and nurses kept reassuring us that I was completely fine; I had no reason to do the C.A.T. scan. In fact, the doctor was filling out the form for us to go home when he stopped, paused for a good while and then said, "Actually, let's get you in for that C.A.T. scan."

Slightly confused but unquestioning, we listened to the doctor and got prepared for the C.A.T. scan. Again, the doctors and nurses assured us that I was fine, this was completely precautionary, it would only take a couple minutes, and then we would be on our way home. My mom even took a picture of me before going into the C.A.T. scan stating, "When will you ever do this again?"

We then waited for the doctor to come back to our curtained off room to tell us, once again, that I was fine. My mom gathered up her purse and stood up as the doctor entered the room, ready to leave. That was until he shut the curtain, looked up at the ceiling and said, "Thank you, Lord, for inspiring me to do that C.A.T. scan." In shock of what he just said, my mom set down her purse, sat down beside me, and held my hand as the emergency room doctor proceeded to tell us that they had found a mass on my brain. The next thing I knew, we were rushed in an ambulance to our Children's Hospital so I could receive emergency brain surgery.

After my surgery, the nurses told my parents to go rest while I recovered and woke up. My mom decided to stop by before leaving and was quite surprised to find me wide awake with a cluster of smiling nurses keeping me company. During this time,

I had a breathing tube in my mouth so I could not talk, but I remembered that both my mom and I knew the alphabet in ASL. This helped me communicate with my mom. When the doctor came in and saw me signing, he was astounded and ordered that I have the breathing tube taken out immediately, because I obviously no longer needed it. When they tried to take out my breathing tube, which everyone reassured us would be a simple procedure, the tube got stuck in my windpipe, causing me to have no air. It was almost five minutes before the doctor frantically ran in and yanked the tube out.

At the first hospital I was treated at, I had very competent doctors and wonderful surgeons, but it felt like they were simply doing their job - there was no joy or heart at the hospital. There was also much difficulty in their failure to listen to me or my parents. You see, when the doctors gave my parents the diagnosis that I had Medulloblastoma, an aggressive, cancerous tumor located at the base of my brain, they were also told that I would need to go through 16 grueling months of radiation and chemotherapy. I would not be allowed to go to school, see my friends, or even be around my siblings because of germs. In addition to this, they gave my parents an excruciatingly long list of all the atrocious side effects that I *would*, not *could*, have.

Thankfully, once they left the room, my mom turned to my dad and said, "This is not our only option, you go find the very best place for our little girl." My dad, being the Stats professor that he is, went out and researched everything he could about Medulloblastoma. He did just as my mom instructed and found St. Jude Children's Research Hospital, where the treatment was half the time with better results.

While I was recovering from my surgery and began re-learning basic things, like how to walk, those who knew me best began calling me "Supergirl." When my parents told me that I had Medulloblastoma I responded by laughing and saying, "That sounds like the name of a supervillain." From that point on, I completely embraced my superhero persona. This significantly helped me, my family, and those around me get through this horrendous experience. I decided that we were actually going to a secret facility known as St. Jude Children's Research Hospital: A place where young superheroes gained their powers and fought to overcome terrible foes, such as the evil "MedulloBLASToma."

I was convinced that the side effects for the treatments were actually signs that I was gaining my superpowers. I was getting X-Ray and laser vision through my radiation treatments. My itchy, sore throat was because of my new fire and ice breath. When I lost my hair, I was actually gaining my shape-shifting ability. The MRIs, where I had to lay still for an hour at a time, became time machines that sent me on an adventure, which I would later report back to my mom.

For every obstacle that I endured and conquered, I received a small "medal" that I would proudly hang from a charm bracelet on my wrist. These became great achievements on my way to my own heroic victory against my great nemesis. By doing these little things, it made what I was going through tolerable and at times even, miraculously, enjoyable! Before I got sick, I was simply playing on the playground pretending to be a superhero. Just a year later I would be facing a real-life threatening villain. Along with all the rest of the little superheroes-in-training, battling by my side, I was now risking my life to contribute to research that later would help save others. Instead of merely imitating a superhero, I was now doing everything in my power to become one.

While going through this experience, I also found that when I looked outside myself and tried to help others, it somehow made everything better. When I found out that the number one fear for children who receive a cancer diagnosis is not losing their life, it's losing their hair, I decided the best way to help those around me was to give out hats and hair clips to these kids.

As I went through treatment in Memphis, Tennessee, I had enormous support from my friends and classmates back home. When I told those that were doing a fundraiser for me, "There are so many kids here that need it more than I do," they all jumped on board and began donating hats and raising money for hair clips for our cause. I am thrilled to say that this little charitable endeavor has blossomed into a non-profit charity called "Hats & Hair from Kids who Care," that has helped over 3,000 children and families in need.

One of my favorite pastimes while at St. Jude was playing kickball on the playground with fellow patients. It did not matter that we were bald, had bandaged arms or legs, wore eye patches, used walkers, or even wheelchairs. We were going to go out and play because we were still kids. I am so thankful that St. Jude realized it was essential for us to do stuff like this. At St. Jude, I could receive the best treatment out there while still being a kid. I am a firm believer that attitude is everything, laughter is the best medicine, and there is a significant difference between surviving and thriving.

After my diagnosis, I was told that I may never walk or run again, that the treatments I would go through would most likely leave me with major learning disabilities that I would have to fight to overcome. But boy did I prove them wrong! I recently graduated from college with my bachelor's degree in Communications. Not only did I graduate Magna Cum Laude, but I did so in only 3 ½ years. I am also happily married to my best friend who I have known, and had a crush on, since second grade. And I can proudly say I am now thirteen years cancer free! Looking back at that little Supergirl, and all that she overcame, it is astonishing to me that I never remember feeling sorry for myself. I just took it day by day, knowing that I would be better one day. I always held on and knew that I would someday get to live out my dreams.

Living through what should have been a nightmare shaped me into who I am today. It has taught me I can conquer colossal adversaries and that when we look around and see how we can help others, we forget the problems we are going through ourselves.

As I look back, I do see both the good and the bad, but the good far outweighs the bad. Even though I never want others to go through what I did, I would not change what happened to me because I wouldn't be who, or where, I am today without it. As I look to the future, I am positive I will be able to triumph over any obstacle thrown at me. Through hard work, creativity, and my own super-powerful will, I know nothing can stop me from scaling my mountains or living my dreams.

"What's Up, Doc?" to NFL

Jojo Townsell

If you ever wondered how one becomes a National Football League player, here is the magic formula: First, you must love cartoons, especially Bugs Bunny and all the superheroes. Then act out those dreams and become a superhero. Next, sign up for Pop Warner football two years in a row and then quit. If you cannot afford football shoes you will have to learn to make an investment in your future. I suggest going to your grandmother for help. She will teach you about hard work by having you remove a whole forest from her backyard. Removing the forest will help you learn to compete in rain, snow, sleet, and mud. When playing your first football game, let the other team intimidate and scare the crap out of you, literally. Then play the entire rest of the game with that extra weight in your pants. Do all these things and more and you too can be awarded an athletic scholarship, play college football, and make it to the NFL.

I played professional football for ten years, and one event in particular stands out to me. It was a beautiful August evening in the New Jersey Meadowlands. I was playing wide receiver for the New York Jets in an exhibition game against the New York Giants. It was an exhibition game, but the intensity was high because the teams were playing for hometown bragging rights.

Late in the game, I was running a called pass route. My quarterback, Pat Ryan, threw the pass high so I had to jump to make the catch. The ball was in the air, and the Giants' defensive backs were licking their chops. A defensive back enjoys the opportunity to tackle a wide receiver when they are not looking, or when they are in the air without the ability to protect themselves.

This is the NFL. Whether you catch the ball or not, defensive players are going to tackle you. I might as well catch it. I did, but one Giants player hit me high on my shoulder pads and the other Giants player hit me low, just above my ankles. My body did a somersault and I fell hard on the artificial turf. It is not as soft as a grass field, and as my head snapped back against the turf, it felt like concrete.

I was somehow able to stand up. I tried to walk, but my legs told me, *You need to sit down because we ain't going nowhere.* I laid on my back until our football trainers came. The trainers started asking me if I was all right. I told them I was. My vision was blurry, and my legs felt weak. I was okay, but it was probably the last play of the game for me. Then the trainers started putting fingers in front of my face asking me how many they were holding up. I looked at them like they were crazy. I answered them so they would shut up. Then they asked me the most bizarre question. "What is your name?" I kept fighting them because they would not take me off the field. I finally answered them, "My name is Horatio."

The Legend of Horatio

Now that you know I once had the honor of being a New York Jet, regardless of my name, it is important to understand what truly is necessary to succeed and become an NFL player. Every athlete has a story that is their best-kept secret. This is mine.

Every Saturday and Sunday growing up, I woke our house up with my impersonations of cartoon characters. When the sun rose, I would be on our porch watching the reflection of my shadow and becoming a superhero. I would extend both arms, flying, as I became Superman, Spiderman, Batman, Aquaman, The Herculoids, Frankenstein, Jr., Thor, or Captain America. I would save my hometown from the evil villains who tried to destroy our neighborhood. Once my shadow was gone, it was time to watch my heroes on television. My fascination with cartoons was not just superheroes; I would also become The Pink Panther, Woody Woodpecker, and The Man: Bugs Bunny. What's up, Doc!?

I am the youngest of seven children: six boys, and one girl. All of us were athletes. It started with my father. Mr. T participated in basketball, baseball, football, and even boxing.

My first athletic endeavor was in track and field - the Junior Olympics in Reno, Nevada, where I was born and raised. The event was held at the University of Nevada campus. I was there to watch my brothers and sister participate. Since my parents were able to get me away from watching cartoons, they entered me into the 100-yard dash. I was seven years old and was used to running races against neighborhood kids in Black Springs, which was ten miles north of Reno. Growing up, I always thought they named the town Black Springs because black people lived there and we all could jump well.

The race was about to start. The other kids were dressed in tank top shirts with club names, nylon shorts, and shoes with tacks coming out of the bottom. I was dressed in a white t-shirt and blue jeans. My mama told me to take my shoes and socks off and run the race barefoot. I started crying because I could not figure out why I was the only boy in the race who had to take his shoes off!! Then Mama said the magic words, "You can be Bugs Bunny." My tears ended immediately, and I was energized to begin the race. Mama always knew.

The starter for the race asked the runners to take their marks. Bugs Bunny did not wear shoes, so I took my shoes off and I was ready! All the runners approached the starting line. I turned back and asked Mr. T, "What am I suppose' to do?"

He told me, "When the starter pistol fires, run as fast as you can."

The pistol fired and the race began. I was running as fast as I could. At the 50-yard mark, there was no one around me. I was winning the race easily. Then for some reason I started running in the other lanes. I started the race in lane one and finished the race in lane ten. The officials were going to disqualify me, but even with this mistake, I won the race by fifteen yards. An official came up and asked, "What is your name?"

I replied, "Bugs Bunny. What's up, Doc?"

I got even more entertaining on the awards stand. I was standing on the top step. An official approached me with a first-place blue ribbon. Suddenly, looking at this blue ribbon, a sense of pride was flowing through my body. I felt important and enjoyed the attention I was receiving from my family and all these strangers. Then it happened: another cartoon flashback. I raised the ribbon high above my head, hearing the cheers from the grandstands, and then I roared, "Bugs Bunny discovers America!" The legend had begun.

Two years later when I was nine years old, it was Sunday morning, which meant Mama made us go to Sunday school. This infuriated me because this meant I only had one day to watch cartoons. Sometimes Sunday school started early, and I would race my brothers and sister home to hopefully watch "The Bullwinkle and Rocky cartoon show."

This particular day, I turned the television on, and the screen showed this man catching a football. Then he high stepped, straight-armed, and juked everyone on his way to scoring a touchdown. Excited, I could not wait for the instant replay to see who this man was. The extra point kick was kicked; then they showed the touchdown replay.

This man was wearing a red helmet with a logo shaped like a tomahawk on both sides. His pants were white with two skinny red lines along the sides. The jersey was candy apple red with white numbers on the front and back of the jersey. Finally, the television announcer revealed, "That was All-Pro wide receiver Otis Taylor of the Kansas City Chiefs who scored the touchdown." Instantly, Otis Taylor became my favorite football player and the Chiefs my favorite football team. I discovered a whole new group of superheroes that would fascinate me along with my cartoon heroes - NFL players. I had never seen a person show the kind of athletic ability that Otis Taylor displayed.

I still enjoyed my cartoons, but you do not have five brothers and not play sports. When cartoons were over, I would always play football, basketball, and baseball with my family and friends in the neighborhood. I started not to mind that football games were being shown on television instead of my cartoons. The first year I started watching football on television, my Kansas City Chiefs beat the Oakland Raiders for the AFL Championship. They were going to meet the NFL's Minnesota Vikings in Super Bowl IV. Super Bowl IV was fantastic because the Chiefs beat the favored Vikings 23-7. The Chiefs' victory not only made me a lifetime fan, but the next fall I wanted to really become Otis Taylor. I signed up for Pop Warner football.

Fall came, I was ten years old and there I was, part of my first football team, the Astros. Yes, the Astros. Mama had bought me a brand-new pair of football shoes, and I was excited to be like my hero, Otis Taylor. There was a lot expected of me because my two older brothers, Duane and Maurice, had become Pop Warner legends. Now their little brother would hopefully have the ability to match their accomplishments. Football practice started, and I found playing football was fun. I could run faster than anybody on the team, and I was better at doing the drills the coaches put the team through. Then, during the second week of practice, the coaches instructed everyone to get in line and receive their football equipment. Football equipment consisted of football pants and pads, hip pads, shoulder pads, and a helmet.

My teammates were trying on their uniforms. They started looking really big with these shoulder pads and the helmets that were hard as rocks. My thought was no way anybody was going to hit me with that stuff! I began to slowly let teammates behind me get in front of me to collect their gear. The line was shrinking, and soon it would be my turn.

The coach yelled, "Horatio, come and get your football equipment." Scared, I did what I had to do.

"Coach," I said, "I need to go to use the bathroom." That was the last time the coaches saw me.

Mama came to pick me up from practice. She asked the coaches, "Where is my son?"

The coaches said, "He went to the bathroom... two hours ago."

Mama went everywhere at Idlewild Park, in Reno, to find me. When she finally found me, I was at the playground, swinging. Mama approached me and asked, "What is wrong, son?"

I said, "Mama, I don't want to play football."

Mama understood I was not ready. She was a little upset because she just bought new football shoes for me, and now they would go to waste.

The next Pop Warner season, I was eleven years old, and I went to Mama and told her I wanted to play football. She gave me one of those looks and questioned whether I was sure about this. I was older and my feet had grown. I was able to convince Mama and she bought me another brand-new pair of football cleats. I was selected to be on the Astros again. The coaches made me feel like last year never happened.

The first week of practice, I was doing great. Like the previous year, I could run faster than everyone and performed well in all the drills. Then that day came when it was time to receive football equipment. I was ready until my teammates began putting their gear on and looked twice as big as they did the year before. Yes, it was time to use the bathroom again.

At least Mama knew where to find me this time. Mama walked up to me at the swing set and I told her, "Mama, I don't want to play football." Yet again, I had wasted another pair of brand-new football shoes, and Mama could see that I most likely was not going to become a football player.

In 1973, I was in seventh grade and went to Clayton Middle School. I did not bother Mama about football. I figured I could watch college and professional players play football on television. I would participate in other sports, particularly basketball. I tried out for the seventh-grade basketball team. This was easy because all my friends were on the team and made me feel comfortable. Plus, I knew my teammates would still look the same when they got their basketball uniforms. I did not run away this time, and I made the basketball team. This made it easy for me to ask Mama to buy me brand new basketball shoes.

My friends and I played basketball all the time. When we arrived at school, we played basketball, at lunchtime we played basketball, and after school we had basketball practice. Our favorite basketball team was the University of California at Los Angeles (UCLA) Bruins. UCLA was coached by the legendary John Wooden, who was making one of the most incredible championship runs in sports history. The Bruins would win 10 national championships in 12 years. My friends: Mike Legarza, David Sutherland, Toby Albin, Mike Arron, and Kyle Saunders patterned our game after the Bruins. We also had success just like UCLA. Our 7th and 8th-grade teams were undefeated in those two years. There were only two times that we did not beat a team by at least 15 points.

My best friend was Mike Legarza. We met in fourth grade at Elmcrest Elementary School. We became immediate friends, mainly because we were the two best athletes at school. We loved sports. Though our friendship was great, there was always a quiet competition between us. For example, we used to play one-on-one full court basketball against each other. Darkness was the only thing that stopped us. The best thing about having Mike as a friend was that we both enjoyed watching college football and basketball. We never imagined playing college sports, but we did see ourselves attending college. To us, college was a way of becoming a success as an adult. This motivation, as we later discovered, was the first goal we ever made in our life. Our goal was to become college students.

It was August 1974; four more weeks of summer vacation and I would be attending high school. I began the morning reading the newspaper. I would read the sports page first, then the front-page news, business, entertainment, and end with the comics. This day, in the sports section of the Reno Gazette Journal, was an article announcing freshman football tryouts for Procter Hug High School, the high school I would be attending. I had gained confidence participating in basketball and track teams at Clayton Middle School. Maybe it was time to give football another chance. There was one problem. I would have to ask Mama to buy me football shoes.

That afternoon, Mama came home from work. I said, "Mama, I want to play football."

She just stared at me like I was crazy. She replied, "Son, you know I will always support you. That is what a mother does. You can play football, but you are going to have to buy your own football shoes."

WHAT! How was I going to pay for football shoes? Fortunately, my grandmother lived next door. We affectionately called her Mama Helen. I asked Mama Helen if she would buy me football shoes. Mama Helen said, "Yes, grandson, I will help you buy your football shoes." I gave her a big hug and kiss and started heading back home.

Right as my foot was stepping out the door, Mama Helen said, "Grandson, you are going to have to do something for Grandma."

Slowly, I turned around and asked, "What is that Mama Helen?"

She said, "I want you to go chop those weeds behind the house."

I knew the weeds she was talking about; they were not simply weeds. Her backyard was a forest! Was football worth it? I decided it was. After two weeks of chopping weeds, Mama Helen approached me and gave me an envelope. I opened the envelope, and it was a check. The check read, "Pay to the order of "the Legend" the sum of $310.67." Mama Helen told me she was able to get the county agency to classify my weed chopping as a summer youth job.

My first job was ground maintenance for the Black Springs Community Center. It was interesting that the community center weeds connected with Mama Helen's forest. Anyway, I was able to work those four weeks and saved $600. I started my first joint bank account with my dad. Mr. T helped me withdraw the money to make my first purchase ever that was not candy. I bought football cleats, and I would be trying out for the Hug High School freshman football team.

The first practice came, and the coaches introduced themselves and gave us the overview of how practices would be.

Among my new teammates, I saw an old friend from the neighborhood named Rodney Hill. Growing up in Black Springs, Rodney and I played together all the time. Rodney was always a better athlete than me. When we were kids, he was the only guy my age that could outrun me and he always beat me in every sport. He was Mr. Football in Pop Warner - the sport I quit twice. His family moved from Black Springs to Reno before I attended Clayton Middle School. Unfortunately, Rodney injured his knee in Pop Warner.

The next time we saw each other was during middle school. He attended Trainer Middle School, and we competed against each other in basketball and track. Two of the games our Clayton basketball team had played in our undefeated seasons were against Trainer Middle School. Rodney was a good basketball player, and we usually guarded each other. Since we won the games, it gave me the satisfaction that I could beat him at something. Then during track season, although Rodney's knee injury had taken away some of his speed and I might have beat him, we never ran a race against each other. This helped me to never lose an individual race while at Clayton Middle School.

When I saw Rodney at football practice, it was nice to see a friendly face. When we began drills, we would be right beside each other. Just like the old days in Black Springs, the silent competition began. Even with the knee injury, Rodney was still an outstanding athlete. His injury helped me to gain confidence that I could measure up to him now and maybe even exceed him in certain areas of competition. Though we competed vigorously against each other, we always had fun and supported each other. Rodney went out of his way to teach me the basic skills of organized football and how to use the football equipment correctly. The main things were to protect yourself when you are running with the ball, and how to block and tackle without hurting yourself. Rodney's friendship and support helped me finally become a football player.

Well, if you can believe it, Horatio was finally playing football and attending high school! In my first year of football with Procter R. Hug High School, I became a starter on both offense and defense. On offense, I was slot back, which gave me an opportunity to both run with the football and catch passes. Defensively, I played free safety. Our first game was against Wooster High School. This was special to me because this was my first official football game. Once the game began, I was kind of in The Twilight Zone. It seemed like I was just another chalk mark on the field, at least until my coaches called "Slot Right 44 Reverse." This was the play for me to run a reverse. The quarterback would fake a hand-off to the running back heading in one direction, and I would come behind the quarterback and get the hand-off and head in the opposite direction.

We broke the huddle, and my stomach was fluttering with 10,000 butterflies. Our quarterback called the signals at the line of scrimmage, and the ball was snapped. I made a quick jab step to the right and then began running left towards our quarterback, Doug Williams, to receive the ball. Doug handed the ball to me and I began to run. Once the ball was placed in my hands, I ran as fast as I could. To my delight, there was only green grass in front of me.

Thirty yards later, a couple of red jerseys approached me. The defining moment was here. The sport of football is not popular because of money or fame. America loves football because of the anticipation of the COLLISION! My first collision was coming. Since I was running near our sideline, I thought I might just take the thirty yards I gained and step out of bounds. No way! It was time to find out what football is all about. It was time to erase the fears of the past. LET'S GO FOR IT!

I decided to stay in bounds. Two Wooster defenders were approaching. Our eyes met and we each silently shouted, "BRING IT ON!" Five, Four, Three, Two, One. BOOM! We had an impact. The two Wooster defenders exploded into my body and knocked me five yards beyond the sideline markers.

I was lying on the ground with the Wooster players. I wanted to make sure my body parts were still there. I began touching myself, feeling my arms, legs, my private areas, and I wiggled my feet. Everything seemed okay. Then I asked my legs, "Can you stand up?" Yes, I stood up. I was all right. I began feeling a sense of pride. The first time I ran with the football, in my first organized football game, I gained 44 yards. I thought maybe that is why they called the play 44 reverse. Anyway, I began to hear the encouragement from my coaches and teammates. I jogged back to our huddle feeling so proud of myself. The Legend is playing football. A superhero is back in the house, again.

The 44 Reverse play helped our offense get in position to score the game's first touchdown. Then Wooster came back and tied the game at 6-6. When the fourth quarter began the game was still tied. Our offense was marching down the field to take the lead. The play came in from the sideline - Slot Right Z Go. This play required me to run a Go route, which is simply to run down the field as fast as you can and catch the football. Doug Williams was a good quarterback and had a strong arm. I did not have to break stride, and I caught the ball and scored the winning touchdown. This was my first touchdown in organized football. The game ended and we had beaten Wooster 12-6. The Hug High School freshman team went on to win the freshman championship with a 7-1 record.

My freshman year in high school sports was fun. Alongside my first year of organized football, I also played varsity basketball and was a member of the varsity track team. I hoped my sophomore year would be even more fun. My hope was answered quickly. Bob Floyd, the varsity football coach, asked my parents if they would approve of me playing varsity football. Mama did not want me to because she felt I would get hurt. I felt the real reason was she did not want me to get in a situation that may raise my doubts and have me end up at the swing set again.

Coach Floyd thought I could help the varsity team. Personally, I did not want to play varsity. Firstly, I wanted to stay with my classmates and play JV ball. Secondly, I had finally overcome my fear of playing football, and I was not sure I was ready for the varsity level. Reluctantly, I became a member of the Hug High School varsity football team. My participation in varsity basketball and track as a freshman helped me believe I could compete with any high school athlete in Nevada. At least this is what I would tell myself to cope with the butterflies every time we practiced. It helped that my freshman teammate, Doug Williams, was also asked to join the varsity team. Well, I made it through varsity training camp and the first game was at home field.

My first varsity football game representing the Hug Hawks was against South Tahoe High School. Doug and I were not expecting to play much. That was all right with me.

The second quarter came, and Coach Floyd yelled at me, "Legend, go in at right defensive back."

I ran onto the field. Wow, my first varsity football action! Things were actually okay. I felt fine but those darn butterflies were not going away. South Tahoe began driving the ball towards our end zone. They had a bruising fullback who, to me, was the Rock of Gibraltar. South Tahoe ran their fullback on a dive play. After initial contact, he broke a tackle and bounced the play outside, and he was running towards me. Oh no, I thought, here comes one of those moments again. Do I have what it takes to play varsity football? Here we go. Five, four, three, two, one...SPLAT!!! I was able to get under Mr. South Tahoe and made my first varsity tackle. Once the play was over, all those butterflies went away. I got up, adjusted my face mask, and headed back to the huddle with my teammates.

Though I was proud I made a play for the team, there was something wrong. Usually, when football players made contact with each other, the sounds are usually, BOOM, OOH, UUGH, YAAH! Mine was SPLAT! While I was jogging back to the huddle, I felt a swoosh slide through my body. Every time I took a step, the swoosh sound was ringing in my ears. Then I realized what happened. My butterflies were free. I had pooped peanut butter stains in my drawers. Damn. At the same time, I felt a sense of accomplishment: I become the original funk master. I played the rest of the game with extra weight in my pants. Finally, the game was over, and we won 20-14. I ran to the locker room hoping to clean myself before someone smelled me. The players and coaches came into the locker room before I could do anything.

Coach Floyd huddled the team together for prayer and a post-game speech. Coach Floyd was a huge admirer of NFL Hall of Fame Coach, Vince Lombardi of the Green Bay Packers. So, his speeches were military. I made sure I was in the back of everybody. Hopefully, no one noticed. Coach Floyd continued his speech, and then he made mention of Doug and I, the only sophomores on the team. He wanted to acknowledge that we were part of the winning effort. Coach Floyd then proceeded to say, "Doug and Horatio were so nervous before the game, they probably crapped their pants." I screamed inside, "How did he know?"

Anyway, we ended our season against the best team that year, Wooster High School. They destroyed us, but I improved as a player. I made ten solo tackles at defensive back and scored my first varsity touchdown on a fumble recovery. My first varsity football experience came to an end. Once I became a professional football player, I became the ONLY NFL player in history who QUIT Pop Warner football twice and started his high school varsity football career with extra weight in his pants. Yes, I became a Superhero.

MARTIN LUTHER KING, JR

When I attended Elmcrest Elementary School, my parents were not pleased with my fourth-grade school performance as a C student. They decided to do something about it by hiring a tutor. They found a young lady who attended Reno High School named Michelle Klaich. Michelle was a nice girl who always had a big smile on her face, a great personality, and made me feel special when we were together. During our time together, Michelle introduced ways that helped me develop better study habits. The main strategies she showed me were how to organize my time after school, complete my homework, and take extra time to understand what I was supposed to learn. Her tutoring helped me take my schoolwork seriously. While I worked with Michelle, my classwork improved, and I began getting better grades. I even started getting A's.

Michelle, an outstanding student herself, was awarded an academic scholarship to Stanford University. When our last session ended, she gave me a huge hug and a gift. I opened the gift and it was a children's book. Up until then, the only books I had ever read were superhero comic books. The book was titled, "The Autobiography of Martin Luther King, Jr.," the great civil rights leader. I thanked Michelle for the book and wished her luck.

I read Martin Luther King, Jr.'s autobiography, in which he detailed how he became the leader of the Civil Rights Movement. The Civil Rights Movement fought for the constitutional rights of all Americans to be treated equally. The movement's ultimate achievement was getting the Civil Rights Bill approved by Congress and signed by President Lyndon B. Johnson on April 11, 1964. Race relations have always been an issue in America. Martin Luther King, Jr. sacrificed his life to make life better for all Americans. When reading his autobiography, there was something more that helped me understand why this man and those before him fought for equal rights. Martin Luther King, Jr. graduated at the top of his class at Morehouse College in Atlanta, Georgia. Then he attended Boston University, where he earned his Ph.D in systematic theology. Dr. Martin Luther King, Jr. was a scholar as well as a man of God.

When I finished reading "The Autobiography of Martin Luther King, Jr.," my first thought was how education was such an important part of Dr. King's life. My second thought was that I needed to set a goal. Something that maybe would make a difference in people's lives, like Dr. King. I remembered what I learned from reading Martin Luther King's autobiography. He believed in education! My goal was to graduate from high school and attend college. This goal was incredibly important to my development. I never knew how important education was regarding participation in school sports. During my middle school years playing basketball and running track for Clayton Middle School, I learned that you could not represent your school in sports or enrichment activities if you were not in good academic standing. My interest in sports helped me to discover that my education was more important than even being an athlete.

If I had not taken my education seriously in middle school, I would not have been allowed to play sports. If I had stopped playing school sports, I would have never gone on to play college football at UCLA or become an NFL player.

My classmates also helped me in achieving my goal. They were good students. We found that we competed against each other in the classroom more than in sports. We all saw ourselves attending college and becoming someone we could be proud of. This association with my friends in middle school reinforced that I had made a good choice choosing education as my goal.

This was just middle school. I would be going to high school the next year and, unfortunately, the friends who helped me excel in middle school would be going to a different high school. I was concerned whether I could make the type of friends in high school who all had the same goal as I did. Fortunately, one of my friends from middle school, Dave Sutherland, also decided to attend Procter R. Hug High School. When I learned that, I knew that high school was going to be okay.

My first day of high school, freshmen had school orientation where we met our counselors and got our class schedules. My first meeting with my counselor went well until I reviewed my class schedule. My class schedule was not what I thought I had signed up for. I wanted to be in a college preparatory schedule. I told the counselor how my goal was to attend college. I asked the counselor if I could change my classes, but it was not going to happen with this counselor.

Whenever I have problems, I go to Mama. Mama would take her problems to her mother, Mama Helen. I was the youngest of seven children. Hug High School got to know Mama Helen up close and in person. Mama Helen was a beautiful lady. She really cared about people and the community. If you got on her bad side, she would curse you out with the best of them.

Mama scheduled an appointment with Hug's principal to discuss my class schedule. Mama Helen joined us. The showdown was set. Whenever Mama Helen went into battle, she would always put her hair back into a bun. She would kind of waddle when she walked, which helped create the scene. That was so that all eyes were on her because you did not want her to have to say it twice. If she had to say it twice, you would feel like ice cream in a cone, lickety-split.

Mama would try to get her serious groove on too! She was standing up for her baby boy. Mama is an angel and has the face to prove it. She makes everyone feel like they are the best piece of cake you ever had. When she tried to look tough, it looked funny. The only time my brothers and sister knew she was serious was when she had a belt, a cord, or a tree in her hand. Old school discipline!

Mama came into the principal's office with her best tough look, her eyes staring fiercely at the principal. Then it was my turn to enter the office. With my family there, I would talk some smack! I said, "We gonna get something done today." But Mama Helen stared at me with that "shut up boy" look. I immediately started looking at the floor and kept doing it the rest of the meeting.

The meeting only lasted five minutes. The Hug High School administration knew that when Mama Helen made a school appearance, she wanted change and this change was going to happen with or without the administration's support. Mama Helen spoke, "My grandson wants to go to college and if you don't place him in the classes that will help him get to college..." There was a five-second pause between her words. Mama Helen's eyes got big and she roared, "I'LL BE BACK!" She turned and waddled out of the office.

It was Mama's turn. She was able to visualize the sounds of lions, tigers, and bears. That helped her explode and say, "YEAHHH!" She walked out with her mean-funny-looking self.

Mama Helen's and Mama's actions brought my eyes from the floor and I looked at the principal. He had one of those looks like he was wondering why he took this job. I seized my opportunity. This was a time I could say anything to the principal and get away with it. I looked at him and said, "That's right! Get with the program or we coming back for you!" I walked out of the office like the school was named after me.

The next day at school, I got asked to come to the administration office.. I was sure the office was going to have their turn and let me know how things were going to be if I wanted to remain a student at Procter Hug High School.

I walked into the office and told the receptionist my name. She politely told me to walk through the hallway, turn left and go to the second office on the right. There was a man in there and after I told him my name, he stood up from his chair and extended his hand and greeted me with a handshake. Then he said, "Hi, my name is Mr. Mike Whellans, I am your new counselor." We proceeded to talk with each other, and we discussed my goal. Mr. Whellans explained what I needed to do and what classes I needed to take every year.

When my parents took the time and money to hire Michelle Klaich to become my tutor, I realized how much my parents cared about my education and my future. I knew I could count on them to give me a chance to achieve my goal. Mr. Whellans gave me the plan to make it happen. I made the most of it. I was not the brightest student, but I did my best. When the first semester of my junior year ended, I found that I had met all the requirements to attend college. I was one year away from accomplishing my goal, a journey that had started in fourth grade because my tutor gave me a book about Dr. Martin Luther King, Jr.

My heroes started with cartoon characters on TV but ended with true-life heroes that I could strive to become more like. From Mr. T. to Mama Helen, my Mother, my tutor Michelle, and all the coaches and athletes who helped push me to succeed. Each of these heroes helped me get to where I am today. Now I try to channel these heroes as I work in my charitable organization I started when I came out of the NFL, MEFIYI (Me For Incredible Youth, Inc.). We help underprivileged kids gain confidence in themselves, set goals, work towards college, and gain what they need to succeed.

Clarity Will Save the World

Veronica Rozenfeld

I am very fortunate to live the life I live today. I mentor owners of multi-million-dollar companies, startups, and corporate professionals, all from home. I am surrounded by loyal and fulfilling relationships. In 2017 Les Brown awarded me the "Most Intuitive Coach Award" after only being in business for 12 months.

A pivotal moment for me was back in 2012 when I was pulling up to a gas station two toddlers in the back seat. This was the first time I experienced what it felt like to have my credit card rejected, once, twice, three times. That is when the reality I was running away from sunk in. I was getting a divorce. Everything I had built was melting away like an ice cream on a hot sunny day in San Diego, California. My financial stability, Russian community, and relationship of 10 years, gone. How did I get to this point in my life? In 1999, at the age of 18, I came to this country heartbroken and unable to speak any English, while also still battling a learning disability. Four years later, I graduated with a degree in Finance and had a corporate job lined up.

However, during this time, I lost myself and was completely unsure of my purpose in the world. I lived what I had believed was "The American Dream". I lived to please everyone else, to meet the standards of my community, and made everyone happy but myself. Something needed to change. I asked myself how I was able to achieve so many goals in four years. The answer is I had a clear vision of what I wanted and had zero attachment to how I would get there. I would show others that anything is possible and help millions of others in the process. And that's exactly what I did. My name is Veronica Rozenfeld, CEO of the "You Rise" Movement. When you clearly know who you are and where you are going, you rise to your greatness and step into your destiny.

Clarity

At the core of my soul, I believe clarity will save the world. When you are focusing on your life purpose and mission, you achieve inner peace. That creates an outer peace with everyone around you. And that is how world wars will be resolved. Environments will react and global warming will dissipate.

Clarity saved my world.

In 2013 alone, I was unemployed six times and lived in fear of being homeless. It was becoming clear that being an accountant with a heavy learning disability was not the path for me. And yet, I did not know what else I could do with my life, accounting was all I knew. That is when I started delving into self-development, energy work, and core entrepreneurial skills that I needed. I wrote a list of the things that terrified me. The list included the fear of driving, running, talking to strangers, and so much more. As I overcame each fear, I learned that fear is a shortcut to our success. I started to build the foundation of the life that was waiting for me.

So, how do you achieve your clarity?

1- Step number one: Figure out your core gifts

Our greatest gifts and skills are always things that come so naturally to us that we tend to take them for granted. We teach people how to treat us, and if we take ourselves for granted, others will too. When I work with my clients to discover what their core gifts are, the most common reply I get is: "Who would ever pay me for that?" My answer is always the same. "Thousands of people outside of your circle. If you're still not sure what that core gift is, find a clarity mentor or outside mentor to get this perspective.

2- Step number two: Figure out how to monetize your gifts

The only reason people are unable to make money on their core gift is lack of self-value. A part of them is not feeling worthy or good enough to get compensated for their gifts. A great mentor of mine once said, "We are wired for greatness, but programmed for failure".

In the first seven years of our life, we are like sponges. We absorb everything around us and thus are creating subconscious programming. Like our cell phones that run the programs that create apps. The challenge is we update our cell phones once or twice a month. How often do we upgrade our subconscious mind? Transforming my subconscious mind helped me turn my adversities into blessings. Now, I am privileged to do it for many others in my business. This concept alone has been able to double and sometimes triple their income in a matter of a few months.

3- Step number three: Create a vision for the lifestyle that you want

We have been taught to make money first, create a lifestyle second. But what if you designed the life you love first and monetized around it? It is important to understand what is essential to you; for me, it is transforming people's lives. It may take a lot of courage and change. But, in the end, spending time on what matters is the most rewarding feeling on the planet. If you do not sacrifice for your dreams, you sacrifice the dream itself. Your dreams could haunt you at night or be the most rewarding reason that gets you out of bed. The choice is yours.

Life is a road of choices. Right now, you are reading this book from a specific address. You know the street number, city, and zip code. When it comes to life, very often we have no idea where we are going. Many of us end up driving 100 miles an hour in the opposite direction- losing time, money, and energy. That is why clarity is the most pivotal and almost always an overlooked part of our lives. I am very privileged in life to find my clarity. That is why I am on the mission to help entrepreneurs and professionals find their mission, vision, and their voice. So that you never have to experience feeling lost, or isolated. The "You Rise" movement is here for you to grow, find your purpose, and find a community of like-minded people. Together, we can find clarity and save the world.

Lessons From Hank

Colleen Butler

In order to discuss how I am mastering my mountains; I need to first describe the mountains I have had to face. Looking back on April 22, 2018, life had been flowing along as smoothly as our chaotic life could expect: hitting the gym 3 times a week, working full time in a demanding job, all while managing a household and 3 children (ages 22, 12 and 10). I was busy, strong and my life was full of goals and direction.

I woke up on April 22, 2018. It was a Sunday morning, and things were as they should be. Getting ready for church, grabbing a cup of coffee, and sitting down with my daughter to watch a few cartoons before heading off to start our day.

This was about the time that everything went cloudy. Literally, I could only see darkness. When I made attempts to focus or see what was in front of me, I was met with a spinning room and bouncing vision. I knew I needed to set my coffee down before I spilled it, but my hands would not do what I was telling them to. I could not think clearly enough to speak and tell my daughter I needed her help.

The mug was set on the nightstand as my hands fumbled. I felt relieved for a moment, then immediately the vertigo-like symptoms took over my body. I navigated my way to the bathroom, bouncing off the walls and barely keeping myself standing. The bathroom floor was my slow landing location. I spent the next hour in this spot with limited ability to speak or think. I also had limited body coordination and felt numbness and tingling on the left side of my face and arm.

Thankfully, my 12-year-old daughter realized something was not right. She found me on the floor and asked if I was okay, while fully understanding something was very wrong. All I could answer was, "I don't think so."

My daughter called my mom, and I could hear the fear in her voice, "Grandma, mom is laying on the bathroom floor and something isn't right."

I was able to send a cryptic text message to my mom, which followed with her arriving at my house in a panic. My 22-year-old daughter had done her research on the way over and was going down a checklist of questions, asking about my symptoms, what I felt, and what I had been doing. The next question was, "Okay, which hospital are we taking you to or, are we calling an ambulance?"

Fast forward to the ER doctor coming in to talk to me about all the tests they had just rushed me through. My mom, my 22-year-old daughter, and my 12-year-old daughter were all hanging out in the room. I expected the doctor to look at me and say she had no idea what was going on and to follow-up with my primary care doctor the next day. She sat down next to me and told me in very clear, calm words, "I'm so sorry, we found a large mass on your brain."

I sat there in shock and disbelief. I remember keeping the smile on my face and saying, "Excuse me, you found what?" She repeated herself, and I looked into the eyes of my daughters and my mom. Disbelief. Pain. Fear. You see, my oldest daughter lost her dad to ALS when she was only 15. She instantly began to hyperventilate and told me, "This can't be happening, I can't lose you."

I, however, never thought anything other than, *this is just a bump in the road, we will get through this*. I told them I was not going anywhere, and we would work through this. I was going to be just fine.

Katie looked at me with tears in her eyes and said, "You always say that Mom. How is this going to be okay?"

I could not answer her with anything other than, "I have no idea, I just know I am going to be fine."

I know in that moment I truly believed I was going to be okay. I knew in my heart and soul that everything was going to be fine. The same as I feel today: it is just a blip on the map, and it is all going to work out.

The days ahead became a whirlwind of research and planning because that is what I do best. I sat down with my family, I called my dad and my sister, explained everything that I knew, and talked through the questions we all had. My mountain seemed to be so large, so scary, but situations like this are what challenge me to find a solution, determine a plan, and execute that plan with a positive outcome.

My mountain soon became mountains, and those mountains became a mountain range as I learned from the neurosurgeons in our region that I was not able to be treated in our area. I was going to have to travel to see a team of specialists for a surgery consultation and treatment plan.

I felt as though the harder I pushed, the more tired I became. My body was losing the ability to adapt and overcome. I was no longer able to navigate stressful situations as I had before. I did not know what to think about this. I did not know how to accept slowing down or having to limit my activity. Many days, I was not even able to drive to and from work.

The months ahead would include so many ups and downs, but a pivotal moment for me happened after Mass one day early in this journey. I was pulled aside by the priest after Sunday Mass as he had heard about my recent situation. He also knew that I was getting ready to travel to California for a neurosurgery consultation. He asked me a few questions, one being how I felt about the travel and the current plan.

I remember feeling emotional and telling him through my tears that I knew everything was going to be fine, some way, somehow, but that I was afraid of the pain of the actual surgery. That was the main thing that scared me. The priest took the time to anoint me with special oils that had been blessed, and he prayed with me. During the prayer, he said something that stuck with me. He said he prayed for forgiveness for me for my fears, along with a bunch of other beautiful words that filled me with strength and more emotion.

After leaving the church, I really reflected on what he said. Even though I had been telling myself I had faith, I believed everything would be fine, and I was praying for strength, I was still filled with fears. The mountains in front of me still felt so overwhelming and I realized I was not truly letting God take control of the situation. I was allowing these fears to control my thoughts and moods. Turning over control to these fears was creating a wall that was blocking actions. Fear is a negative reaction, and I needed everything positive in front of me.

I did not know how to handle struggles when they were my own. I was good at managing and problem solving for everyone else at work and at home. I was good at being the rock for my children and working hard to make life happen and get things done, but here I was faced with having to ask for help. Physically, emotionally, financially, and spiritually. I felt as though my life was starting over.

Everyone's mountains look very different. I do not believe we are meant to move the mountains out of our way; instead, we should be taking the hands of our community, our family and friends, our support, to help us up the mountains. To navigate them and celebrate the highs and the lows. To learn from the journey along the way. When you witness another climbing with grace it inspires you to do the same, or at least ask more questions and observe the climb. How and why are they doing what they are? What is my why? How do I find that strength? Maybe she will hold my hand too. This is how I envisioned my journey at that point. A strong tribe of women, daughters, mothers, sisters, and friends turned into my tribe of strong people. A line of us holding hands and making our way over this treacherous mountain. It never seemed to be unachievable because the moments that I felt the weakest, someone else stepped up to hold my hand.

I have asked so many questions of myself during the last nine months, some I received answers to, and some to which I am still waiting and looking. I keep learning though, and that is what is important. I firmly believe that taking a positive attitude has paved the way for my battle and recovery.

What have I learned, and what will I do with what I am learning? The harsh reality is taking time to realize that not all people can handle the journey. I have lost friends along the way. My fiancé even walked away because the stress of the unknown was just too much for him to bear.

Some of my friends have told me that they are scared to talk about my brain tumor or my health in general. They have said this is because they do not know what to say or they are afraid of *my* what-ifs. Instead, they just stay away. I have learned to forgive those that are unable to emotionally deal with my situation. I do not take their feelings personally nor do I accept their inability to cope as my own. Just because they are afraid does not mean I have to be.

So, the people that I initially felt I had lost, are not so very lost. It is an opportunity for growth. I have a choice; I can sit back and do nothing, or I can reach out and educate, forgive, and move forward. I pray for those that need the strength and understanding. I reach out to them and see how they are doing when they are too afraid to reach out to me.

One of the tasks that has been my greatest therapy during this time has been to blog my thoughts, feelings, lessons, and medical journey. My form of blogging has been social media for now, but as I have the energy, I want to begin a formal blog. This therapy is what led me to write this chapter, my lessons, my journey, and my life.

You always hear that laughter heals, right? More than ever before I have been in tears and laughing all at the same time. Another lesson- allowing the tears to flow and cleanse your soul is a beautiful thing. Feel the emotions and embrace them. Just do not continue to live there. Feel them, allow them, do not feel guilty because of them, and then move on from those sad, fearful, or anxious thoughts. It will not change anything to stay in that frozen state of fear.

You are the only one that can make the choice to change your perception. Sometimes, this means not understanding all the why's and the what's. Sometimes, it means praying for understanding and healing from those fears, and the strength to make the choice to have hope. For me, this means finding the reasons to smile and laugh, creating an environment of positivity and sharing it with others.

At one point early on in my diagnosis, I was trying to explain the status of the large mass on my brain to a friend. I said I was not going to allow this to control my life and take away my happiness, and I did not want to continue to refer to it as "the tumor" or "the mass." That sounded so negative to me. And although I do explain it in that way at times, I do not give that tumor the power to take away my hope. I told my friend I needed to give it a name so we could refer to it as something else. I was telling her that the tumor was not encapsulated like a cyst, it was more of a sticky substance spreading out with tentacles wrapping around the carotid artery and nerves and pressing on many sensitive areas of my brain. She burst out with, "HANK! We need to call it Hank. You know, the annoying seven tentacle octopus from Finding Dory?" This resulted in a pretty fantastic giggle between the two of us, and from that day forward, we called it Hank.

How has this been helpful? In so many ways, it takes a very serious situation and gives it a much lighter side. My kids can laugh a little when they tell their friends about Hank in Mom's head. My posts on social media that relate to my thoughts or education on medical situations start with "Lessons from Hank." By naming it or referring to the tumor in a more visual and relatable way, this has empowered me and given me hope.

When I feel confused or overwhelmed, I cannot always speak the thoughts going on in my head, or I stutter, and my words freeze up. Sometimes I am just forgetful. When my family or friends look at me with confusion, or they are waiting on me to say something, my reboot is simply, "Dang it, Hank!" I take a big deep breath, close my eyes, and try to start over. Sometimes we all burst into laughter and move on to another topic entirely.

I have had times when I was unable to verbally communicate, not really understanding why, but I was able to simply say the word, "Hank." This is the cue for those around me to know something is not okay. I have since learned that some of my episodes are seizures, and the vertigo that follows these episodes is the fog after a seizure. I do not mind making a joke about those moments and laughing through the frustration. It is in those moments, the scariest storms, that I see light and find the direction I need to go.

Since I started posting my Lessons from Hank, I have had complete strangers recognize me in our community and come up and let me know how much they appreciate my faith and positive attitude, or that they are praying for me every day. Imagine my confusion when they say this to me.

The first couple of times this happened, my first thought was, "What are you talking about, and how do I know you?" Then they explain they have been following my inspirational posts. So many have thanked me and said that even though they may not comment, or I may not even know they have read the post, they wanted me to understand that it was the boost that kept them going that day. A smile when they did not have anything to smile about. A reminder to fight when they did not feel they had anything to fight for.

They're finding strength through someone else's challenges and how they choose to overcome their own mountains. I find healing and strength through knowing that I have offered another person the gift of faith, strength, hope, or joy. My gift and my strength come from those moments.

My youngest daughter wrote me a note one day and it said this: *Mom, thank you for being so strong and showing me what strength is. No matter what you are always here for us and I love you for that.* My middle daughter is always the first to step up and help those in need. Even through our daily struggles she says, "Mom, we have a loving home and we should open it to more children that don't have a home or a family." She does not identify our challenges as something negative. She is aware that we have many blessings to be thankful for. My oldest said to me, "You are my rock; you aren't allowed to go anywhere. You have to be okay. Always."

I know that God has given me life and He chose to place me on this path for so many reasons but raising three beautiful humans with hearts of gold has been the biggest blessing He could give me. I will learn to compensate for my physical and cognitive challenges. I know that all I have worked for in this life was not in vain, and that being a leader for my girls is enough. I know that God's love and forgiveness is enough and that I am worthy to be happy and fight a graceful battle.

For those that tell me they are sorry for what I am going through, or share their anger because I have to climb the mountains, I tell them it is okay. I am thankful for all of this. I have learned to be humble, to slow down, and ask for help. I have taught my daughters grace and how to be strong in the face of what seems to be a challenge or task without a solution. I have learned to show kindness in the middle of adversity.

God will always show up and show us the way. He will always provide. I have learned to live my life not just speaking the words but living them as well. When it feels overwhelming, that is usually the beginning of the biggest blessing.

I used to be so afraid of the dark. I was afraid to walk through the room without a light on, venture outside at night, tackle scary changes, or to shed tears in front of a room full of people. I know now that overcoming these fears is not a solitary journey. I am bringing precious people along with me. We are growing together, and I thank those who reached out their hands to walk up the mountain by my side.

I have learned that decluttering and removing the negative in my surroundings will be my most profound accomplishment. I have had to learn the difference between planning and control, and that I am not always in control of everything that is going on. And I am okay with that. I can tackle the little bits of planning. I make my to-do lists and check them off as I go, but understanding that I may not be the one to complete all those tasks has been the toughest lesson to master! I am not always in control.

Sometimes my lines are blurry; this is referring more to the blurred lines of mutual respect and community support. I think we tend to compartmentalize our giving, or our support for those around us. I hear this all the time, "How is that going to benefit me?" "What will I get in return?" "I can't." "That sounds like a lot of work." or "But this is how we've always done it." I could go on for days on this subject. My point is that it is okay to blur the lines, think outside the box, and embrace the changes. Sharing in a task and working together in what some perceive as unconventional ways can be okay!

In your community, should you not reach out and open the door for someone simply because they are a human and standing in front of you? Would you look at that person and draw a line to the entrance of the grocery store? Telling them you will not open the door for them, but you will for the next person? Does that accomplish your goal of sharing a positive experience or helping someone master a mountain?

When you allow yourself to accept the blurry lines, it does not mean that you agree 100% with that situation, it means that you are willing to share your soul. That you can be the person to offer a happy moment for someone that may not have as many happy moments as you did that day. It means that you take a step away from judgement and a step towards healing. Inspire others to see and live past the lines that have been drawn in the sand. Jump right in there and build a bridge right in the middle of it!

If I said, "I can't," every time I had a challenge in front of me on this crazy journey, I could not imagine what my world would look like today. I do know that it would not be as filled with love and forgiveness as it is right now.

I challenge each of you to take a moment and say, "I can." Take a moment at least once a day to take one extra step forward. Do not draw that line in the sand, but hold someone's hand and help them across the line. Make your lines a little blurry, and then watch how many mountains you will overcome as a result!

From Hopeless to Ooh Raa

Joel Peterson

In 2015, when my mom moved in with me to feed me by hand for almost a month, that is when I learned that in the first three years of my life, neighbor's and family had to donate blood to keep me alive. I was projectile vomiting and had a blood disorder that took traveling to many specialists to figure out.

At 4 ½ years old, I was put on Ritalin, and by 5 years old, I was on Cylert. To this day, I still do not remember most of my youth. I was that hyperactive child who was always in trouble and being held after class. Growing up with Attention Deficit/Hyperactive Disorder, and being sick through my youth, was a shock to my system. I had an incredibly difficult time in school, and had trouble interacting with other students and people in general. My mother even had a hard time with my ADHD and took me off my Ritalin by the age of 12. I felt completely different than others. I was never told or taught about ADHD and did not remember being medicated for it in my youth, but at the same time, I knew something was wrong.

Since school was so difficult for me, my mom gave me sage advice that I still remember to this day, "Son just get D's, and you will still be the first person in our family to graduate high school."

I believe this is the only reason I graduated, because it lowered my stress level enough to actually complete twelve years of school. In 1986, at the young age of 17, I joined the United States Marine Corps. I became a Heavy Machine Gunner, and we were the first ones to drive Hummers. I was different even in the Corps, and many knew it.

I did two tours in Okinawa, Japan and training in South Korea. We later were involved in the MAU-SOC, Marine Amphibious Unit, Special Operations Capability. I received an honorable discharge in 1990, two months before the official start of Desert Storm. Now as I look back, I realize I joined the Marine Corps to show my fathers, (step and biological) that I was a man. They were both extremely strict, physically and verbally abusive fathers, whose approval I ambitiously sought.

After being honorably discharged, I knew things had changed. I started taking classes at a university, and amazingly, I ended up on the President's Honor Roll! Shortly thereafter, I began experiencing serious back pain, which kept me from completing school and made it impossible to work. I even tried to rejoin desert storm, but was told no, due to being on the President's Honor Roll. They said there were plenty of Marines sitting on their a**es, and I needed to stay in school. I remember going home really ticked off, told my dad, and he said, "You did your time, let others do theirs." The VA considered me disabled and gave me a 10% disability rating for my lower back.

They put me on Vicodin, Flexeril, and Soma. This led me down a 24 year stretch of depression, pain, suicidal thoughts, and eventually full disability... In 2014, my thumbs started to go numb and this is when I finally reached out to the Reno Veterans Affairs. It took months to get an appointment. After many months of tests and labs, they started hinting that it was in my head, that I needed to quit stressing, and I just needed to eat more. I had dropped down to 135 lbs. and had to check into and E.R. to get help. I felt I had gotten lost in the system.

In 2015, while holding my head up, my mom would have to feed me by hand, because I was too weak to feed myself. I was not sleeping and had to count sheep or count anything for that matter just to keep a rhythm of breathing. This is when I first experienced what I believe was life threatening anxiety, however I did not know it at the time. Sometimes I would only eat two to four pieces of something simple like meat or potatoes, maybe a couple pieces of vegetables and a little bit of milk.

I knew I was dying, and so did my mom; I could see the look on her face. On our way to the VA, mom went grocery shopping, and a lady saw the fear on my face while I was sitting in our car, unable to help my mom with groceries, and she gave me the name of a local acupuncturist and asked If I had thought about holistic natural medicine. To this day, I consider this lady an angel that came out of nowhere. I reached out to my nephew and asked him if he would help me buy a phone so I could go online and study more about nutrition. This is when I started to learn about the absolute corruption in American Medicine, American food, pharmacopoeia, vaccines, and insurance. This is when I was told about Whole Foods, Natural Foods, and the Great Basin Co-op. People at these stores started to know of my story, and they became, in many ways, my doctors and nurses. They were the only ones willing to help as they knew without them, I would die.

Tara Finley was the local acupuncturist that specializes in Oriental medicine and she started to treat me. The problem was I trusted the VA, and I was not getting better, even though her acupuncture helped me just get by. One day while yelling at God, I realized, *"Hey, you're still yelling at God, which means you're still alive!"* This hit me like a rock. In that moment, I felt that He may actually be listening to my prayers, even when I was cussing at him. I believe this is when I experienced my first post-traumatic growth, which is caused by true faith and hope, and I finally let myself start to believe that I might actually live. While shopping at Whole Foods, I stumbled upon *Healthy Beginnings* free magazine and this is where I found Dr. William Clearfield's phone number, and I reached out to him. He's a doctor of osteopathy (DO), and this is when my Whole Foods friends told me and I quote, "If you stay at the VA, and on your same path, you're going to die. You've got to get to a new doctor." In my mind, breaking away from the VA was like breaking away from the United States of America. It was an extremely difficult choice, but it is one of the reasons I survived. Doc reassured me and ran his tests/labs, and anywhere from 7 to 12 days later, we got the results back. They showed my testosterone was extremely low, he gave me a shot that day, and the color came back into my body. He then recommended quality supplements, told me what foods to avoid and what to start eating, and he started acupuncture twice a week on me. I believe this was the most pivotal part of the process in saving my life.

One day, I showed up to an off-site VA auditory hearing appointment, and it had changed to a vision site, so I missed that appointment. I walked over to a Tandy Leather Store, as I always had an interest in leather. The owner, Mike, came over and started to talk to me and let me know he was a Vietnam veteran. As I started to tell him some of my story and what was going on, he referred me to Kary Fritz, the recreational therapist at the Reno VA Hospital. I did not want to have anything to do with the VA Hospital by now, as I had my own private doctor and barely could afford him, but something still told me to go. So, one day I showed up after a night of anxiety and thinking about returning to the VA. I had multiple problems with the VA going all the way back to 1990 when I first sought help, and was put on Vicodin, Flexeril, and Soma. I met Kary Fritz, and she said to come to her class at the VA to see if I would like it.

Some of the Vets at the class came over, and introduced themselves, and gave me some encouragement. I started pounding on a little round piece of leather to learn how to work and engrave the leather. As you can imagine, when the next class was going to happen again, my fear and anxiety started up. I remember thinking to myself, do I really want to go to the VA? I thought I was done with the VA, and was so mad at the VA, but I decided to take that next step, little did I know, this was my first step to mastering my mountain.

I decided to go to the Therapeutic leather class, and within the next couple months, I had learned of a teacher that saved the leather program at the VA. Her name is Tina Drakulich, and I reached out to her. I volunteered to help her make combat paper out of used combat uniforms, as she is a Gold Star Mom who formed a nonprofit, after her son who was killed in combat, known as The David J. Drakulich Foundation for Freedom of Expression. After 24 years of disability, this was my first time getting out of the house (besides going to the VA), and I started working with Tina Drakulich on Sundays. This turned into 5 hours of work every Sunday, and one and a half hours of leather on Mondays. Little did I know that after 24 years of being homebound on disability, this would be exactly what I needed. It gave me the courage to ask around about other volunteer opportunities. One doctor I was seeing off and on said no, as he was afraid of liability. So, I asked Dr. Clearfield if I could volunteer for him, and he said, and I quote, "Well why wouldn't I let you do that. Of course!"

I started volunteering for Doctor Clearfield, and this allowed me to work in an environment without the stress of a regular job. He did not mind if I did not show up, and I didn't have to give him a certain number of hours or show up at a certain time. I did not have to let him know when I was going to be there, and he did not bother me at all; instead he started mentoring me. He is one of, if not the most honest doctors I have ever met. I have seen dozens upon dozens of psychiatrists, psychologists, and doctors over my lifetime. I started volunteering for Dr. Clearfield, and he started to compensate me with supplements. This helped with the cost of having a private doctor. I then began to go outside of the office, and I started to feel the urge to tell people about this great doctor and what he was doing to help me feel better than I had for so many years. This led me to 1 Million Cups, an entrepreneurial group, where companies give their pitch and the audience critiques them. Through this, I joined a business consulting group and became an advocate, consultant, researcher, speaker, and writer for veterans, as well as first, second, and third responders. I also now advocate for the 14 out of 21 veterans who SUCCUMB to suicide every single day in the United States of America who do not reach out to the VA Hospital. I understood because I too was very mad at the VA and did well over 360 videos going off on the VA, allopathic doctors, and local advocates who I believed were not doing their job. Everyone at the VA started to reach out to me, and say, "You know we are veterans too, and we're dealing with the politics of the United States government. We are doing everything we can to help."

Because of this outreach, I started to hang out more at the VA. This is when I started to gain friends back; it's as if my comrades had come back into my life. I got asked to be a volunteer at the VA Hospital and ended up becoming a volunteer under the director of the Reno VA. I then was asked to join the Veterans Mental Health Council Board and the Veterans Family Advisory Board. After being on these boards, I started to experience the politics of the VA, and this is when I started Consulting and Advocating for the Veterans I had come to know.

I realized there were a lot of myths, lies, and bad politics at the VA. I also learn about the men and women dying of suicide that do not utilize the VA. This set me out on a quest, one step at a time to figure out why they left their brothers and sisters behind. As veterans, we have this tendency to stay together, and just stay with the DAV, Amvets, American Legion, PAV, VFW, Rotary Club, etc. I also noticed a lot of my brothers were not at the entrepreneurship groups that I took part in. This is when I saw a possibility to link these groups together. I have now given away 1000 business cards as the professional patient, with my phone number and email on them. Many people now want to work with me, as I'm working/volunteering for Dr. Clearfield, the Drakulich Foundation, and the VA. This has allowed me to mature in a professional manner and helped me to deal with my discoid lupus, Gulf War Illness, Post Traumatic Stress/Disorder, and so many other illnesses and physical ailments.

There are many veterans who are disabled and fighting for their lives. I believe well over 100,000 have now succumbed to suicide in the past nineteen years that we have been at War. I believe that these suicides are preventable. Suicide ideation is physical it is, not merely mental. I experienced suicide ideation my whole life. I thought it was normal and everyone thought this way. Now after eating proper organic food, taking the proper supplements, doing bio-identical Hormone Replacement Therapy, and getting off the 13 pills that the VA had me taking (up to 34 times a day), this has allowed me to realize that I no longer think about suicide ideation. My TBI, which expresses itself as ADHD, PTSD, Anxiety, Major Depression, etc., has been stabilized. Yes, I said stabilized! So now, I advocate that suicide ideation, anxiety, depression, post-traumatic stress disorder, is physical, not mental.

This to me is pivotal because it allows the veteran, first, second, third responders, and their families to have hope! I believe understanding that sickness is physical, not mental, will lower the suicide rate in our country. Many believe their depression, anxiety, PTSD, ADHD, etc., needs to be medicated for the rest of their lives based on psychiatry and psychologist recommendations. I work with a doctor that fixes your hormones and stabilizes you with proper labs, not labs paid for by pharmacopoeia, insurance, vaccine manufacturers, and the United States government (aka political medicine.) That is why he is called a private doctor, and we now have treated many employees and veterans who have also stepped away from what I call political medicine at the VA Hospital. These veterans are getting better, which allows them to climb their own mountains. We plan to bring these testimonios to light.

I now have been coached, consulted, mentored and schooled by many. I am honored and privileged to be asked to become a Score mentor for veterans, and I now sit at the tables of some of the mentors who were once mentoring me. I have created a platform on Facebook where I am maxed out with 5000 friends, and my last birthday 364 people wished me a happy birthday! I have a following, which to this day still has me in awe! Being disabled for 24 years, I have experienced years where no one wished me a happy birthday, not even my mom and dad, because for us it was just normal not to. For over seventy percent of my adulthood, I did not have the ability to take care of myself and had to move in with my parents.

I now own my own home, and still volunteer for Dr. William Clearfield, the David J. Drakulich Foundation for Freedom of Expression, the Veterans Mental Health Council Board, and the Veterans Family Advisory Board. After 24 years of disability, I now get out in public and volunteer. Many of you who are disabled can take your first step at volunteering, just like I did! With 21 veterans and responders killing themselves every single day in America, you too can make a massive impact just by volunteering. This literally can save a life.

I know this, because I have now responded to six suicides myself and am suicide assist qualified. We veterans are known for not leaving anyone behind and this is why I research so many hours 6 days a week. I believe I can provide solutions on suicide and sickness through our Hub of Hope. I now bridge that gap between private doctors and the VA/regular Hospital doctors. I used to get upset at the lab people, but now they understand Dr. Clearfield's request for specific labs, and they work together. This took years for that trust to be built. I now have a way to spread this knowledge to other VA's and private doctors throughout

America. We now have the Choice Program, and I believe its name has been changed to the Mission Program. This allows veterans to go outside of the VA Hospitals to get help.

I have been developing ways that veterans can volunteer and help their local VA, while also helping their local private doctor; that's right, I said help their local private doctor. Because as your professional patient, I advocate, consult, research, speak, and write on behalf of veterans, first, second, and third responders. This includes doctors, nurses, social workers, police, firemen, EMTs, Marshalls, Highway Patrol, state troopers, counselors, teachers, dispatchers, family caretakers, and many more. Doctors are now succumbing to suicide at a greater rate than veterans. Doctors are killing themselves at 40 / 100,000, and veterans kill themselves at 30 /100,000. This is a physical sickness in America, and I believe it's brought on by major corruption, poisons, toxins, pills, vaccines, genetically modified synthetics so-called 'food', the insurance industry, and moral injuries, which are all backed or overlooked by the United States government! The above is why I believe these veterans and responders need to heal and become the people they once were before they got sick. If I can get rid of my own suicide ideation and stabilize all my sicknesses, then so can you!

We all must take the next step, one person, one organization, one VA/Hospital, one church, one art/therapy program at a time.

I am now a leather Smith, and part of the Reno Veteran Photography Group, (another VA recreation therapeutic program.) I have also received a guitar for being in the veteran guitar group at the VA Hospital. We have fly fishing, bowling, and some even have golfing. We also have an art class that my father, who is 74, is now part of and it is changing our lives. All these programs are allowing us to receive therapy at the VA Hospital, all without pills.

This false perception and belief that Suicide Ideation is mental has many believing there is no hope because you will have to take pills the rest of your life. Many scientists, researchers, and universities around the world are now learning it's physical! We now know it is what you eat, pills you are taking, or have taken, past beliefs, and your social influences that can lead to suicide! I used to say Dr. Clearfield saved my life, (which he did), but now I see that taking that step that next morning out the door, is also what really saved my life. I'm always going forward and working through the fear of not knowing what's going to happen. Many thought I would not be here by now, after 5 years. Lipodystrophy is in a classification of HIV known as AIDS. Discoid lupus can turn into systemic Lupus, and these are deadly diseases. Many call these autoimmune diseases. The definition of autoimmune disease is your body attacking itself. Just like I do not believe suicide ideation is mental, I also do not believe the body attacks itself. I believe this autoimmunity classification is wrong, and now believe the body is lacking enkephalins, endorphins, proper nutrients, and proper hormonal balance. The connection between the brain, heart, and the gut is actually what will heal us.

I tell people if you go into a desert with 120-degree temperatures and do not drink water for 4 days, you will lose your mind. You do not lose your mind because you are weak and because it is mental, you are losing your mind because your body isn't properly hydrated, which is physical. Hormonal and nutritional deficiencies cause a similar physical reaction that allows your mind to lose its ability to think, and many have killed themselves because of this. I am here to tell you that I believe when you are able to figure out what is wrong and stabilize your body, you will also stabilize your mind. It is not the other way around, and this is being proven worldwide.

One day while going to another conference, (Nevada Osteopathic Med Association) with Doc and the other DO's in town, a well know doctor from California by the name of Sam Donaldson gave a presentation on suicide! He was talking about the pills that can help suicide and I will never forget Doc leaning over and saying, "He is not even mentioning hormones, he is going straight for the pills. He supposedly is one of the best doctors in the country on suicide!" This was one of those conferences where the doctors must give a class on suicide and ethics every year to get recertified. I have the privilege to show up at these events and listen to anywhere from 4 to 8 doctors in a day give their presentations on what they believe and perceive. I walked out that day asking Doc why did I not kill myself after being so sick my whole life and going through what I did between 2014 and 2015? It hit him pretty hard too, so we reached out to another doctor by the name of Mark L Gordon in the millennial Institute. He is known as an Interventional Endocrinologist. He started a program that measures and stabilizes brain hormones.

Dr. Clearfield became the first doctor in Nevada to be certified in this process, and this led us into traumatic brain injury. We now believe TBI is one of the main causes of anxiety, depression, and what many call post-traumatic stress/disorder. I always wondered why so many non-combat veterans were coming back with post-traumatic stress. I now believe TBI, moral injury, multiple exposures (pills, Vaccines, poisons, toxins, GMO food), are the main reasons. TBI can be caused by visual stimulation, not just physical impacts, but it also can be caused by what you perceive, what you believe, and what you were exposed to/taught at a very young age. This form of trauma you experienced at a young age happens with your Delta and Theta waves. We now balance the hormones between the pituitary gland and the hypothalamus, which allows you to balance the rest of the hormones in the body. I believe this has helped change Dr.

William Clearfield's practice and his personal beliefs on suicide ideation. We now understand it to be physical. With what I've learned, along with being a grunt in the United States Marine Corps, I now have the tools to help others break free from TBI/post-traumatic stress/disorder, anxiety, depression, manias, attention deficit hyperactivity disorder, and many other so called mental disorders!

I actually believe I'm experiencing post-traumatic growth, aka PTG! PTG is part of the new sciences known as Neuroscience, neuro endocrinology, and psycho-neuro-Immunology! We now believe you can regrow your brain cells, even after combat, explosions, toxins, poisons, cancers, etc. that you have been through. There are now ways to fix all the above. We believe those ways are natural from nature: natural food, natural hormones, natural supplements, proper cognitive EMDR, biofeedback, Peptides, Stem Cells, Exosomes, unconventional therapies, all are means of correcting yourself.

This is a stark contrast between showing up at a psychiatrist or a psychologist office and talking your way through what you perceive as your own problem, and then receiving pills. Many psychiatrists and psychologists believe you will be this way the rest of your life. I have experienced this perception throughout my life, and now knowing it was, and is physical, is how I mastered my mountain! I now take no prescription Rx! Back when I started this journey, I never said, "OOH RAA," I now say "OOH RAA" all the time! We have a saying that is known worldwide, "Once a Marine, always a Marine!" I understand that is not always true, because for a time I gave up on being a Marine. I will never again give up on my fellow Marines, or my brothers and sisters from all the other services. I am a United States Marine, who is also Your Professional Patient!

Love Like It's Your Job

Jeff O'Neal

Being diagnosed with Stage Four Colon Cancer and given just 3-4 months to live on March 24, 2016 has definitely impacted my perspective on life. I have always believed life was about relationships, whether it is with my Savior, wife, kids, parents, family, or friends.

I remember, soon after my diagnosis, walking through my house while everyone was asleep. I looked in each room and thought about how blessed I am. My children's lives, their character, their compassion for people, and if they have received salvation through Jesus to me is essential to my success as the head of my home. How I love my wife and helping her find her strength, and to realize her value as a child of God is critical to my success. It is my job to provide for my family and give emotional security to each of them. My most important role is to love my family, my friends, and lead by example on how to serve others. I believe my wife and my kids reflect this and it makes me incredibly proud.

I believe God has me on a path, and I know my family will watch to see if my actions reflect my words and my beliefs. I commit to go through my cancer journey with great faith and transparency. I will have bad days or weeks as I start treatment, and that is okay.

I started to think about my oncologist's statements to me that were very discouraging, and I am not going to act like I was not in a bad spot. However, I get frustrated when people do not believe in the power of prayer, or that God can move mountains. There are accounts in the Bible where God healed the sick, made the blind see, turned water into wine, and even raised a man from the dead. He can surely heal this body, and that is what I am praying for every day. Whatever God's plan is, we will praise Him as He is worthy to be praised.

After my first round of chemo, I became extremely sick with fevers, and I was admitted to the hospital to be watched overnight. After this round, I began to have sores in my mouth and my feet were dry and cracking. According to my wife, the skin around my eyes was sunken, and my eyes were yellow. I had no energy and I struggled to get off the couch. My heart was not functioning well, and my liver constantly shot pain through my body. I knew that this was not going to be good for me. Since the beginning of this journey, I have trusted God - even if that means I do not beat this cancer - because he is my Savior. I live for Him, and I will not fear anything.

After my first round of chemo, my friend who I have known since high school - as she and her husband were my young life leaders - introduced me to a very potent alternative treatment plan. The team behind these powerful nutraceuticals told me that these nutrients may be able to help me to rebuild my cells faster than the chemo could tear them apart.

After three weeks of taking them, about 90% of my side effects were gone. I have been playing half-court basketball, my hair is growing faster than it ever has, I have so much energy, my appetite is great, and I have no pain in my liver. Doctors told me I did not have much chance to beat this cancer, but I am not only surviving, I am thriving. I continue to be blessed with very minor side effects from the harsh chemo I am on. I am still able to live life and enjoy the blessings God has bestowed. Getting a death sentence from a doctor is difficult, but we are all dying. We just do not know when. This journey has shown me God is in control, and I need to trust His plan.

If I can ask a favor, please consider your perspective on life; it changes everything. This is difficult for me at times, but it is a good reminder. When the kids are hyper and not listening, or your teenager - who is hormonal and trying to figure who they are - makes you crazy, consider it joy because God blessed you with children to love and raise. When you get frustrated at your job because people can be difficult, consider it joy because you are physically able to work and provide for your family, and many people would love the opportunity. When your spouse makes you frustrated because as humans, we tend to be selfish and want our way, thank God because He blessed you with somebody to spend your life with.

My heart is humble, I feel peace, I love my new life, and I am thankful for the blessing of this cancer. I would not miss this for anything. Man can say your days are numbered, but the creator of the universe knows us intimately, and it is His will we seek. My hope is in the Lord, not man!!!

During this journey, I was having a procedure done, and I got frustrated with the lack of faith they kept casting on me, so I decided to put a mask on to keep germs away and wrote on it "1 John 3:18" and the words "LOVE LIKE IT'S YOUR JOB." God sent a nurse in, and we talked for about 10 seconds. I knew in her smile she was different, and something was special about her. She asked me about the verse and the words on my mask. I shared a little bit about my faith, and she shared a beautiful story of a life redeemed by the Father, despite the doctor's assessment. At that moment, I asked her if I could pray for her. God's got this, and he reveals himself daily and I never want to miss it. My nurse, myself, and my wife have become great friends and our families have become close as well.

I want to share a story of a 22-year-old girl that I worked with as a probation officer. She was addicted to heroin; her boyfriend, who got her pregnant, was the dealer, her mom was not a positive influence as she was a user, and her dad was not an influence at all. He was not a user, but he did not encourage his daughter.

This girl met with me monthly, but as I took time to get to know her issues, she began coming in my office almost weekly for encouragement. I kept tabs on her in her drug program, and we tapered her off heroin by using the methadone clinic. She gave birth to a baby who was taken by CPS. She wanted to give up, but she kept believing and trusting what I said. I worked with the social worker, who was excellent, and saw the girl working hard. She got off methadone, she had custody of her baby, and control of her drug problem. She even took a leadership role to other females in the program because she believed in her worth and she was not going to let somebody have that negative influence on her again.

It would have been easy to write this girl off, but many times these are the ones that just need someone to say, "I got you, let's do this together." I hope this comes across as intended, not about anything I did, but a young girl with great potential who simply needed someone to say, "I will see you through this, you can do it." God just happened to put me in that situation. Never underestimate the impact you can have on another if you simply care about them more than you care about yourself. This young lady overcame her fears and pushed through.

At the beginning of this journey, I shared my personal motto: Love Like It's Your Job! To me, this defines my rescuer personality. I want to love others always and make them feel cared for. That means everything to me. Loving others must be part of who we are.

Years before my diagnosis, I dealt with depression and anxiety due to a work environment that was incredibly difficult to handle. I was under so much stress, and I struggled to function. I barely spoke to my wife and kids unless I was yelling. I always seemed to be on edge, hated going to work, and I took it out on my family. I remember sleeping in my game room just so I could avoid talking about my stress and how work was affecting me. I really damaged my relationship with my wife and kids, especially my daughter.

After dealing with the depression for almost two years and being able to recognize what was happening, I struggled to pull through it as I could not find my joy or hope, despite God blessing me with a great family. My son kept asking me to go to the boys' youth group on Monday nights as he wanted me to be involved. I knew God was using him to push me in the right direction, but I wanted to isolate, and it was more comfortable to withdraw. I went with my son, but I was hit and miss for quite some time. When I went, I loved being with these youth boys and mentoring them, loving them, and being loved by them.

As my perspective shifted, and I gave all of myself to these boys and then the youth on Wednesday nights, my depression changed, and I was blessed more than anything I could have imagined. I felt a calling to youth ministry as a leader, and I had a passion again. When you give, you receive more than you even realize.

Thanks to cancer, I am off work and have been able to connect with the kids and spend time together, which would not have happened otherwise. This cancer has been a blessing in so many ways. My son and I are much closer, and there has been healing from the damage I caused a few years ago when I failed to recognize the plank in my own eye. My wife and I are closer now than ever before because we came together to battle this cancer and trust God. Without this cancer, I would have never experienced the joy and love for others, from others, and in others. Consider it all joy when you go through trials and tribulations, as God uses it to draw us close to Him.

The first couple of months of my diagnosis, I would lay in bed in the mornings, at night, and whenever I needed to focus on the Lord and listen to a special song by Jeremy Camp called "Same Power."

The first verse about the "waters raging at my feet," I saw as my cancer trying to overtake me. The next verse about the "breath of those surrounding me and nations rising up," I pictured all the friends and family standing with me in prayer. As the next verse says, "we were not going to be overtaken." I viewed this as nothing would shake my faith and that I was trusting the Lord with everything, no matter what happened.

The following verse about "walking down this dark and painful road and facing every fear of the unknown" is my favorite verse. With God by my side, and surrendering completely, I would face this painful road of cancer treatments and not fear the unknown, for my God is with me.

The next verse about "all God's children singing out we will not be overtaken," I pictured people wholeheartedly praying for me and asking our father for a miracle.

The verse after talks about the power in us through the power of our God. "We have hope that his promises are true, in his strength there is nothing we can't do." His word is true, and I know if He wants to heal this body, despite what man says, IT CAN HAPPEN! "There are greater things in store" could be an eternity with Jesus, but I believe that because of my situation, people came to Christ, and God is using this situation in ways I do not see to further His kingdom.

The verse "greater is He that is living in me, He conquered our enemy. No power of darkness, no weapons prevail, we stand here in victory," says there will be victory in Jesus, regardless of what happens to me. The Lord has touched so many through this cancer, it must be victory.

This song got me through many days at the beginning, and I still sing it daily. The Lord will not always give us what we want, and people die daily, and it is hard to understand. We are not in control; this is God's plan, and we just need to be thankful for the days we get. Being angry and bitter just forces us to miss out on the blessings.

I can easily feel sorry for myself, have a pity party, and ask everybody to feel sorry for me. I could justify being angry, isolating myself, and closing out everybody. Stage 4 with a 2% chance of surviving 5 years is bad, but it could be worse. If I get so caught up in what is not going my way, I will not realize all the beauty in front of me.

When I was born, my parents were told there was a chance that I would not survive. At age 15, I had an accident which caused me to go blind in one eye. Facing adversity is nothing new, but it is how I face it that means everything! I do not know how much time I have here on Earth, and it does not matter. I am trying my best to love others, help my wife realize how strong she is - which is amazing to watch - share about what Jesus did for us and how it matters, and probably most importantly to me, show my kids how to face the most difficult situation with courage - trusting God every step of the way - no matter the outcome. I want this diagnosis to shape them, and I know they watch everything I do as to how I handle setbacks. I make mistakes daily, but I never quit, and I never blame God. This has been the greatest year of my life.

Do not spend time worrying; it just steals your joy. Life is short, with or without cancer. I am living my life to spend eternity in Heaven.

"Now I want you to know, brothers and sisters, that what has happened to me has actually served to advance the kingdom." Phillippians 1:12

Jeffrey Sean O'Neal went to be with the Lord February 18, 2018. Look for his wife Kim O'Neal's upcoming book "Nothing but a Blessing" as she shares about Faith, Hope, and Love during Jeff's cancer battle, along with other life struggles.

***

Jennifer Baker is an internationally recognized Business and Motivational Speaker, Executive Coach, a Master Certified Expert for Digital Marketing, business and political consultant, and the creator of the Success GPS Programs and Seminars. Jennifer was invited to co-author an overnight Best-Seller, "The Road to Success" volume 2 with Jack Canfield in 2016 and launch in 2017. Jennifer has been selected as one of America's Premier Experts™, and internationally recognized as one of the Top 100 Most Influential people from Influence Magazine. Jennifer spends her time speaking to, training, and supporting tens of thousands of companies that range from start-ups and 'Dream-preneurs' to Fortune 100 companies worldwide, and has multiple awards from the most important people in her life as Best Mom in the World. She 'retired' in her 30's from her executive-level position to pursue her purpose to helping others create a positive life of balance and impact. Jennifer shows her clients how to increase success through ethics, values, socially conscious efforts, and business development so they have enough money to live the life they want and still be able to be a good parent or mentor for the next generation. Jennifer is passionate about helping businesses and executives create a positive ripple effect in business and professional climates, which is the best support for our nation's economic and family stability.

***

Tamara L. Hunter *is the President and Co-founder of Chemo Buddies for Life (CB4L.org), a 501c3 nonprofit with the mission to end isolation during diagnosis, treatment, recovery, and the "new normal" life due to cancer. A survivor herself, she has heard, "You have cancer" far too many times. She is now building a worldwide movement that supports both the patient and those who care for them. CB4L.org believes in healing through connections within yourself, with a "buddy or buddies," and with a strong community that shares humor, heart, hugs, and a whole lot of love. CB4L.org has found a unique way to support programs and systems that are making a difference for those who have been utterly underserved throughout the United States. Now, CB4L.org is expanding and growing, reaching "buddies" located in many countries throughout the globe. Tamara won "The First Next Global Impactor" competition on August 30, 2019. A competition that looks for people who are ready to take their message, cause, or mission to impact the world. The creator and host of The Service Hero Show, Tamara celebrates service three times each week. Now in her third year, Tamara is committed to sharing, "Inspiring Stories of Those Inspiring Others." She believes, "We all have a Service Hero inside." On August 28, 2020, Tamara L. Hunter joined the e360tv Web Tv Platform with her show, and it can be seen live on millions of screens internationally.*

***

Craig Nielson *serves as a coach, motivational speaker, and advocate for women. He specializes in coaching women to become fully empowered by building stellar self-confidence and breaking down all barriers of insecurity and self-doubt. At the age of 21, he was hospitalized for three weeks for severe depression. From that very dark place in his life, Craig made a full recovery with professional help, exercise, and finding healing in the Gospels, along with the love of God's grace. During a 13-year career in law enforcement, Craig worked with victims of sex crimes, domestic battery, and sexual assault. Wanting to work more proactively to help people, he returned to school to earn his master's degree in Counseling and Educational Psychology. While counseling college students, Craig noticed a common thread with many female students suffering from low self-esteem and poor self-image. From there, he knew his collective life experience had prepared him for his true calling: coaching women to become fully empowered and fearless. Today, Craig lives a positive and healthy lifestyle in Reno, Nevada with his wife of 24 years, daughter, and son. Craig is an avid runner and has completed 5 marathons, including the prestigious Boston and New York City marathons.*

***

Kim O'Neal *is 44 years old and lives in Visalia, California with her two children, Nick (20), and Natalie (16), and their German Shepard Nala. Kim was blessed to have been married to Jeff O'Neal for 22 years before God called him home at the young age of 44. Kim wears many hats in her life from being a stay at home mom for 18 years while helping raise 28 foster children. She volunteers in her church as a youth leader and a leader in the college department. Kim also serves on the women's ministry team and has begun to share her story with other widows. Kim is also certified with HELM to help educate. She teaches and shares with others how our bodies can be healed through nutrition and about powerful nutraceuticals that have helped so many. Kim loves to travel, be outside, laugh, hanging out with her kids and their friends, and just enjoying every day God gives her. Kim has begun her dream of sharing her story of how God can turn your worst into something beautiful; she will continue to share and live her husband's legacy. Kim always goes to Jeremiah 29:11* **"For I know the plans I have for you declares the Lord, plans to prosper you and not to harm you."** *Look forward to her upcoming book:* NOTHING BUT A BLESSING.

***

Chase Marmolejo *is from California's Central Valley. She has a bachelor's degree in Communications and Digital Film from DSU, St. George, UT. She is a Brain Cancer Survivor of 13 years and has been a spokesperson for Make-a-Wish, Childhood Brain Tumor Foundation, and St. Jude Children's Research Hospital over the past 12 years. She has participated in numerous events to promote and raise funds for these wonderful charities. She is also the founder of the Non-profit, Hats & Hair from Kids who Care, which gives out hats, hair clips, and comfort items to children with life threatening illnesses. She is currently working toward becoming a sign language interpreter. She is the author of the children's book "Vella Novella: The Book That Talks Back", a book for anyone ages 6 to 106. She is an avid reader and loves Fantasy. When she is not reading or filming her Chase the Fiction Fanatic vlog on Youtube, she enjoys watching movies, playing board games, and riding roller coasters whenever she has the chance. She is happily married to her best friend, Tristin, whom she has had a crush on since second grade. And she hopes to one day own a puppy with him. Look for her next book in The Books that Talk Back series: Fact & Fantasy.*

***

JoJo Townsell is living an amazing, fulfilling life in Reno, NV, where he was born and raised. Joseph "Jojo" Townsell begged his grandmother to buy him shoes so he could play football. Then after getting signed up and starting practice, he decided maybe football just was not for him. At that time, his mom and grandmother instilled in him that once he started something, he was to see it through. He would later become a talented high school athlete who would be highly sought after. He would eventually end up playing first at UCLA, and then as a wide receiver for the New York Jets in the National Football League, which is a phenomenal accomplishment. After retiring from the NFL, he has dedicated himself to helping others. This is where he has attained his most extraordinary achievements. "Great leaders don't set out to be leaders, they set out to make a difference. It's never about the role-it's always about the goal." After moving back to his hometown of Reno, Jojo began working with at-risk youth helping them see their own phenomenal potential. His non-profit organization is MEFIYI. (Me For Incredible Youth, Inc.)

***

Veronica Rozenfeld *was raised in Russia and moved to the United States at a young age with very little English and a dream. After working as an accountant, she finally found her true passion, helping others find their highest self and live their best lives. It was her work with a fourth-generation healer and internationally recognized physicist that helped her master the Diamond Method. The unique process combines energy work, clarity guidance, and vision building to help everyone who goes through this process live the life of their dreams. Today, Veronica is an internationally recognized transformational intuitive clarity mentor. She has worked with start-ups, business entrepreneurs, corporate professionals, business leaders of multi-million-dollar companies, and everything in between. In 2017, she received the Most Outstanding Life Coach & Intuitive Energetic Healer award. She is a founder of the YouRise movement and is committed to bringing people back to their power, back to their life path, and aligned with their most fulfilled and happiest version of themselves.*

***

Colleen Butler *was born and raised in Alaska and now lives in Nevada. Retired mom to three beautiful girls with an extended family of dogs, cats, and chickens. She currently keeps busy homeschooling her two teenagers. She made the transition from grant writing and management to writing about her experiences with a life changing diagnosis. Colleen is a brain tumor warrior, finding strength through her journey by sharing her challenges and triumphs with others, actively reaching out, and encouraging those that need a helping hand or an uplifting story. Positive words, faith without fear, and always imagining herself healthy inside and out, Colleen continues to inspire all those around her to conquer the battles they face and master the mountains they must climb.*

***

Joel Peterson *was born and raised in Sacramento, California. The first 3 years of his life, family and friends had to donate blood to keep him alive. He joined the United States Marine Corps at 17 years old and was honorably discharged in 1990 after serving in the 3rd Battalion, 3rd Marines. By 1991, he was in college and on the President's Honor Roll. Soon after, his back gave out, and Joel was no longer able to work. During this time, he became severely depressed and suicidal. In 1994, he checked himself in, as a VA impatient, for drugs and alcohol. He stayed in this program until 1996, when his twin sister died in a horrific car crash. That year he had to mature and raise her son, his nephew, which he did until 2012. By 2014, he was horribly sick and only weighed 135+lbs! He eventually was diagnosed with discoid lupus, lipodystrophy, Gulf War Illness, traumatic brain injury, and post-traumatic stress disorder, with mania and major depression. He sought help in the VA and finally went to a private doctor named William Clearfield, which saved his life. He started to volunteer under Dr. Clearfield, at the Reno VA under the director. He then volunteered for the David J. Drakulich Foundation for Freedom of Expression, the Veterans Mental Health Council Board, and the Veterans Family Advisory Board. For the next 3 years, he set out on an entrepreneurial path and his entire life changed. Joel became an entrepreneur, advocate, consultant, researcher, speaker, photographer, and an inspirational healer. He now advocates, speaks, writes, researches, and consults on behalf of the 14 out of 21 veterans who succumb to suicide daily in America. He believes that we need to be there for our brothers and sisters, because an American Veteran leaves no one behind.*

***

Jeff O'Neal *was a loving husband, father, son, and friend. When Jeff was given a diagnosis of only a few months to live, he never gave up hope and was determined to fight. Jeff's faith grew and he began to turn his struggles into joy. He became an inspirational speaker and started to change lives through his pain. Jeff was married to Kim O'Neal for 22 amazing years, and his pride and joy were his two children Nick (age 20), and Natalie (16). Jeff was a probation officer for 21 years and he loved helping the kids that needed help the most. His passion was to help them see they have a future and help them accomplish their dreams. Jeff served as a youth leader at his church where he became a second Dad to so many. He also served on the non-profit sports board at his church where they helped kids in the community play all kinds of sports. The field that these young athletes still play on is now dedicated to him. Jeff grew up as an only child in a small town in Exeter, California where he raced BMX bikes, played high school basketball and tennis, and excelled in all sports. Jeff's two passions were playing basketball with his son, Nick, and watching the Denver Broncos. Jeff may not be with us today, but he leaves behind a legacy that only grows. His inspiration for teaching others to LOVE LIKE IT'S YOUR JOB will never be forgotten. Because of all the beauty he saw during his cancer journey from people accepting Christ, marriages being saved, Fathers stepping up and being Dads, and people just doing what is right in this world, he would say, "I consider this cancer nothing but a blessing." Jeff will always be missed but never forgotten. "Now I want you to know, brothers and sisters, that what has happened to me has actually served to advance the gospel." -Philippians 1:12.*

132

Jennifer Baker

My humble acknowledgments:

To my champions who refuse to let me call them by name, you've shown me what love, commitment, dedication to doing good, and what true strength through illness and adversity really looks like. YOU are my heroes and I feel so blessed to understand the 'real' in reality through you. To the most amazing heartfelt publisher who lives in service to her beliefs, faith, values, family, and friends, thank you, Season Burch, for being a steadfast rock and for sharing love through real-life everyday heroes story's. Most of which would never be told if it weren't for your pleasant nudging and passion for humanity.

To Nathan and Mikayla, my heroes and favorite people on earth. Thank you for stepping up to your path of purpose early in life. Thank you for blessing my life and for being uniquely YOU. Our lives have not been easy and will continue to challenge us, sometimes at levels that we believe are unbearable. They are worth every second with you! Thank you for continuing to take on life with such incredibly fierce love, passion, discipline, and conviction.

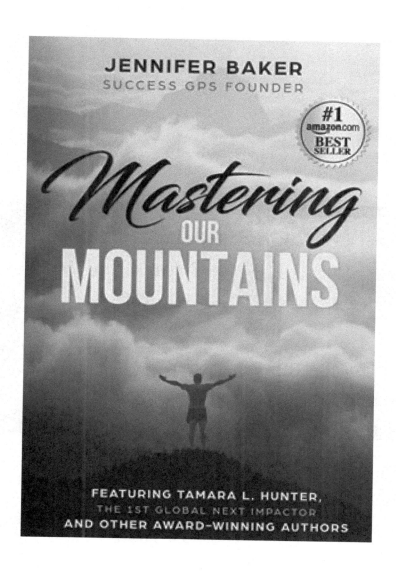